797,885 Books
are available to read at

Forgotten Books

www.ForgottenBooks.com

Forgotten Books' App
Available for mobile, tablet & eReader

ISBN 978-1-331-59920-3
PIBN 10211049

This book is a reproduction of an important historical work. Forgotten Books uses
state-of-the-art technology to digitally reconstruct the work, preserving the original format
whilst repairing imperfections present in the aged copy. In rare cases, an imperfection in
the original, such as a blemish or missing page, may be replicated in our edition. We do,
however, repair the vast majority of imperfections successfully; any imperfections that
remain are intentionally left to preserve the state of such historical works.

Forgotten Books is a registered trademark of FB &c Ltd.
Copyright © 2015 FB &c Ltd.
FB &c Ltd, Dalton House, 60 Windsor Avenue, London, SW19 2RR.
Company number 08720141. Registered in England and Wales.

For support please visit www.forgottenbooks.com

1 MONTH OF FREE READING

at

www.ForgottenBooks.com

By purchasing this book you are eligible for one month membership to ForgottenBooks.com, giving you unlimited access to our entire collection of over 700,000 titles via our web site and mobile apps.

To claim your free month visit:

www.forgottenbooks.com/free211049

* Offer is valid for 45 days from date of purchase. Terms and conditions apply.

Similar Books Are Available from
www.forgottenbooks.com

Beautiful Joe
An Autobiography, by Marshall Saunders

Theodore Roosevelt, an Autobiography
by Theodore Roosevelt

Napoleon
A Biographical Study, by Max Lenz

Up from Slavery
An Autobiography, by Booker T. Washington

Gotama Buddha
A Biography, Based on the Canonical Books of the Theravādin, by Kenneth J. Saunders

Plato's Biography of Socrates
by A. E. Taylor

Cicero
A Biography, by Torsten Petersson

Madam Guyon
An Autobiography, by Jeanne Marie Bouvier De La Motte Guyon

The Writings of Thomas Jefferson
by Thomas Jefferson

Thomas Skinner, M.D.
A Biographical Sketch, by John H. Clarke

Saint Thomas Aquinas of the Order of Preachers (1225-1274)
A Biographical Study of the Angelic Doctor, by Placid Conway

Recollections of the Rev. John Johnson and His Home
An Autobiography, by Susannah Johnson

Biographical Sketches in Cornwall, Vol. 1 of 3
by R. Polwhele

Autobiography of John Francis Hylan, Mayor of New York
by John Francis Hylan

The Autobiography of Benjamin Franklin
The Unmutilated and Correct Version, by Benjamin Franklin

James Mill
A Biography, by Alexander Bain

George Washington
An Historical Biography, by Horace E. Scudder

Florence Nightingale
A Biography, by Irene Cooper Willis

Marse Henry
An Autobiography, by Henry Watterson

Autobiography and Poems
by Charlotte E. Linden

QUEEN AND CARDINAL
A MEMOIR OF ANNE OF AUSTRIA AND OF HER RELATIONS WITH CARDINAL MAZARIN

BY MRS. COLQUHOUN GRANT

AUTHOR OF "THE FRENCH NOBLESSE IN THE XVIIITH CENTURY," "A MOTHER OF CZARS"

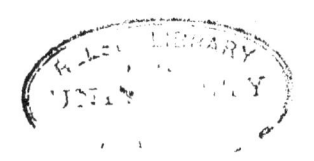

WITH PORTRAITS

LONDON
JOHN MURRAY, ALBEMARLE STREET
1907

PRINTED BY
HAZELL, WATSON AND VINEY, LD.,
LONDON AND AYLESBURY.

PREFACE

IN the following account of the life of Anne of Austria I wish at once to disclaim any idea of posing as a writer of history. The period embraced by the memoirs of this remarkable woman—one of the most important Queens-Regent who were ever called upon to act the part of a sovereign—is a very attractive one.

The alliance of Bourbon and Hapsburg initiates a new era, in which dynastic considerations are all-important, but the larger facts of the histories of France and Europe in the seventeenth century have been treated by many able historians, and do not enter into the scope or intention of these pages.

I have dealt mainly with the life of Anne of Austria in the more intimate details of her home life, and of her court filled with attractive women who were by turns her friends and her enemies, and only one chronicler is to be found who throws any light upon the subject from this point of view. This is Madame de Motteville, the Queen's faithful bed-chamber woman, who wrote four volumes of memoirs, well known in France, though but little read in England. I have endeavoured to cull the more interesting portions from this book, which was compiled—if not during Anne's lifetime, directly after her death—by the one person competent to speak of the *vie intime* of this Queen who lived two hundred and seventy-five years ago.

On one subject, however, the De Motteville Memoirs are silent. No mention is made of the deep attachment existing between Anne and the famous Minister, the Cardinal Mazarin. Respect for her royal mistress, and regard for her fair fame, caused Madame de Motteville to preserve a discreet silence. Other contemporaneous writers were, however, by no means so chivalrous. All the memoirs of the time treat of this famous love-story as a veritable *chronique scandaleuse*, and the question as to whether a private ceremony of marriage had taken place between these lovers was raised, but never satisfactorily settled. Be that as it may, the fact remains, that into Anne's sad and lonely existence a great romance entered at a time when her youth and beauty had waned and she had already attained middle age, and it lasted till the end of her days.

It is more particularly this episode that I have tried to portray in these pages, in the hope that the picture of the loves and sorrows of famous personages in the far-away past may prove of interest to the readers of to-day.

The student of history must turn to other and cleverer writers if he wishes to study France at that epoch.

C. GRANT.

DINARD, 1906.

GENEALOGICAL TABLE

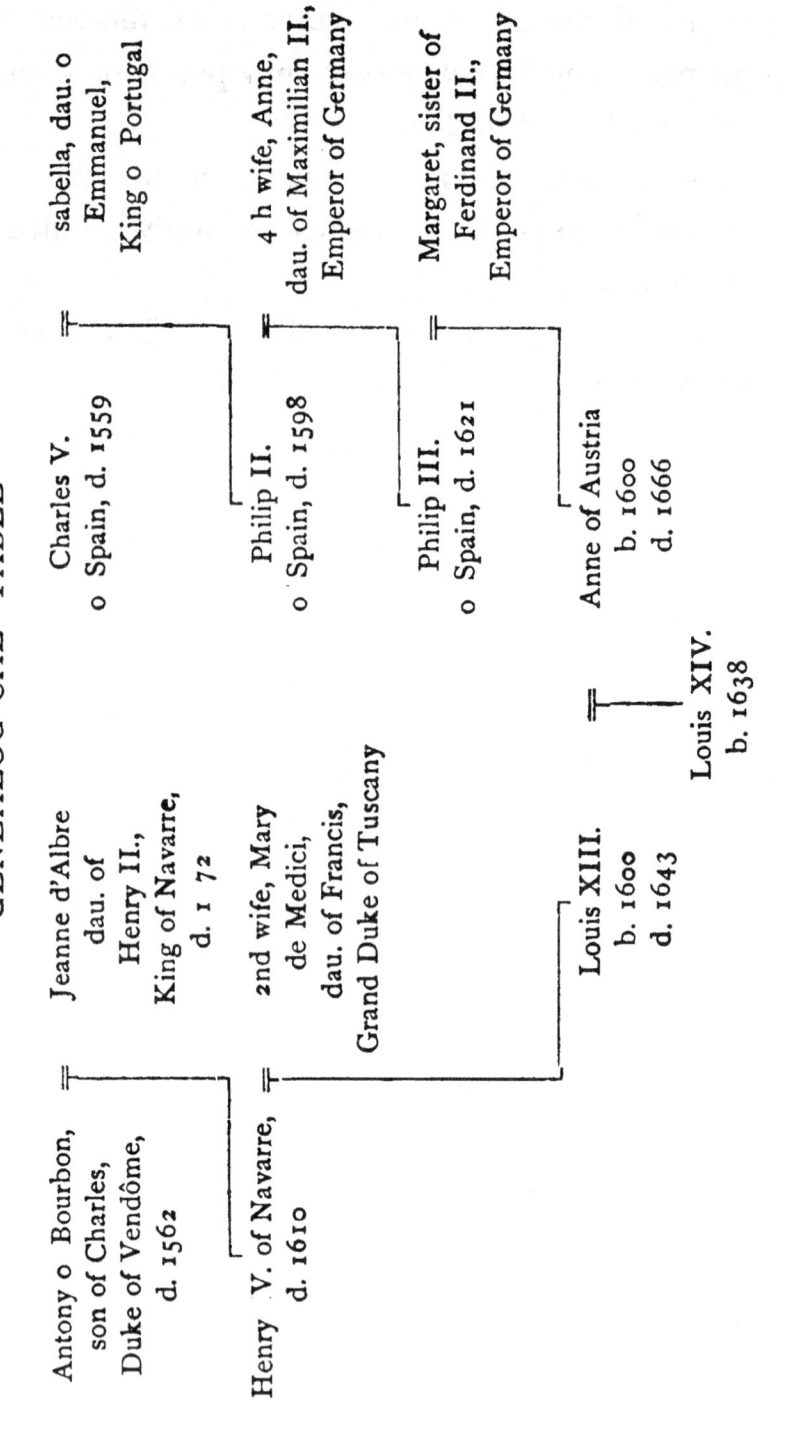

```
Antony o Bourbon,  ═  Jeanne d'Albre         Charles V.      ═  Isabella, dau. o
son of Charles,       dau. of                o Spain, d. 1559    Emmanuel,
Duke of Vendôme,      Henry II.,                                 King o Portugal
d. 1562               King of Navarre,
                      d. 1 72
                                     │
                                     │
Henry V. of Navarre,  ═  2nd wife, Mary     Philip II.      ═  4 h wife, Anne,
d. 1610                  de Medici,          o Spain, d. 1598   dau. of Maximilian II.,
                         dau. of Francis,                       Emperor of Germany
                         Grand Duke of Tuscany
                                     │
                                     │                Philip III.     ═  Margaret, sister of
                                     │                o Spain, d. 1621   Ferdinand II.,
                                     │                                   Emperor of Germany
                                     │
                          Louis XIII.     ═      Anne of Austria
                          b. 1600                b. 1600
                          d. 1643                d. 1666
                                     │
                                 Louis XIV.
                                  b. 1638
```

CONTENTS

CHAPTER I
THE MARRIAGE OF LOUIS

Two Young Princesses—The Spanish Bride—Royal Preparations—The French Bride—The Interchange—Louis XIII.—His Occupations—His Letter of Welcome—Description of Anne—An Unlucky Omen—The Marriage—Anne's Difficult Position . . . .

CHAPTER II
THE INFATUATION OF BUCKINGHAM

Duc de Luynes—Duchesse de Luynes—Anne's Flirtations—Duke of Buckingham—The Royal Banquet—Court at Amiens—Romantic Adventure—The Duke's Farewell—His Audacious Conduct—Last Interview—Cardinal Richelieu   14

CHAPTER III
RICHELIEU INTERVENES

A Love Intrigue—Richelieu's Accusation against Anne—Marquis de Chalais—His Death—Exile of Duchesse de Chevreuse—Siege of Rochelle—Unhappy Union   26

CHAPTER IV
THE QUEEN AND THE COURT

Val-de-Grace—Archbishop's Visit—Court Beauties—Marie de' Medici—Queens reconciled   35

CONTENTS

CHAPTER V
THE "COUP DE COMPIÈGNE"

Queen's Bed-chamber—The Queen-Mother—"Coup de Compiègne"—Return of the Duchess—Her Midnight Visits—Chevalier de Jars—Hangman to the Cardinal—Scene at the Altar—De Jars condemned and reprieved . . 41

CHAPTER VI
THE POWER OF RICHELIEU

Adventures of the Duchesse de Chevreuse—Arrival in Spain—Richelieu's Power—The Unhappy King—A Slave to Richelieu 52

CHAPTER VII
MAZARIN

Mazarin's Parentage—Mazarin's Youth—His Passion for Gambling Mazarin's Relations—The Violet Robes—Anne and Mazarin—Raconteur and Wit 58

CHAPTER VIII
THE CONSPIRACY OF CINQ MARS AND DEATH OF RICHELIEU

Birth of the Dauphin—Marquis de Cinq Mars—His Arrest—Cinq Mars executed—Death of Richelieu—The Two Ministers 66

CHAPTER IX
DEATH OF LOUIS XIII. AND RISE OF MAZARIN

Death of Louis XIII.—Louis XIV. enters Paris—Interview with Mazarin—Anne Queen-Regent—The Vendôme Cabal—Le Petit Conseil—Mazarin's Advice—Marquise de Senacé—Duchesse de Chevreuse—La Belle . . . 73

CHAPTER X
MAZARIN AS MINISTER

A Love Letter—Quarrel of the Ladies—Le Jardin de Renard Indignation of Anne—Les Importans—Flight to St. Malo—The Duel—Court Moves to Palais Royal—Mazarin's Power 84

CONTENTS

CHAPTER XI
THE QUEEN'S LIFE AS REGENT

Anne's Daily Life—Le Grand Cabinet—The Queen's Supper—Her Religious Observances—Summer at Rueil—Mazarin's Illness—Anne's Devotion to him 94

CHAPTER XII
THE QUEEN AS REGENT

Return of Henrietta Maria—Battle of Nordlingen—The Parlement—Lit de Justice—Anne consults Mazarin . . 102

CHAPTER XIII
MARRIAGE OF PRINCESS MARIE

Marie de Gonzague—The Envoys from Poland—The Marriage by Proxy—The Queen of Poland—Her Arrival at Warsaw—King Ladislas—A Dearly-bought Crown 108

CHAPTER XIV
GROWING ATTACHMENT OF THE QUEEN AND CARDINAL

Anne's Love of the Theatre—Education of the King—The Italian Troupe—The Cardinal's Grand Ball—Scandalous Insinuations—Anne questions La Porte and learns the Scandal—The Queen's Oath—The King has Small-pox—His Recovery 116

CHAPTER XV
MAZARIN'S PALACE

His Art Treasures—His Library—Mazarin's Luxury—The Retiro—Mazarin's Ascendancy—Supposed Secret Marriage—Mazarin's Faithful Love—His Dominion over Anne 127

CHAPTER XVI
GATHERING STORMS

The Cardinal's Nieces—Twelfth Night—Mazarin's Revenues—Anne offends Mazarin—He counsels Prudence—Riot at the Notre Dame—Captain of the Guard dismissed . 136

CONTENTS

CHAPTER XVII
MAZARIN IN DANGER

Arrest of Broussel—A Tumult ensues—Broussel released—Terror at Court—The King leaves for Rueil—The Court returns to Paris 144

CHAPTER XVIII
THE FRONDE

Midnight at the Palace—Anne's Flight—Discomfort at St. Germain—The Fronde—Queen of the Frondeurs—Hatred of Mazarin—Distress in Paris—No Peace, no Mazarin—End of the Fronde 151

CHAPTER XIX
THE AFFAIR OF THE MARQUIS DE JARZÉ

Poverty at Court—Mademoiselle de Chevreuse—Madame de Chevreuse coldly received—Marquis de Jarzé—Meeting in the Garden—Duc de Beaufort's conduct at the Supper—The Cardinal's Jealousy—Waiting-woman dismissed—Insult to Jarzé—Condé takes his Part. 161

CHAPTER XX
DISAFFECTION AT COURT

Fickle Parisians—The Tabouret—Revolt of the Nobles—The Queen in Difficulties—Anne sends for the Bishops—Mademoiselle de Montbazon—The House of Rohan   172

CHAPTER XXI
THE YOUNG FRONDE—RESIGNATION OF MAZARIN

King and Queen at Rouen—Escape of Duchesse de Longueville—Tempest prevents her Sailing—Mazarin surrounded by Enemies—He resigns the Charge of the King—His farewell to Anne—He decides to leave France 180

CHAPTER XXII
MAZARIN IN EXILE

Mazarin's Flight—Excitement in Paris—De Chauvigny holds Office—Mazarin still pulls the Strings 188

CONTENTS

CHAPTER XXIII
THE CARDINAL'S CYPHER LETTERS

PAGE

Cypher Letters to the Queen—Expressions of Love and Unfailing Devotion—Letter No. 3—Letter No. 31—Letter No. 34—Letter No. 43—Letter No. 53—Letter No. 63—Letter No. 74 Letter No. 96—Cardinal about to return—Unbroken Union 193

CHAPTER XXIV
THE RETURN OF MAZARIN

Intrigues among the Ladies for Mazarin's return—The Grand Monarque—Chateauneuf as Minister—Duchesse de Navailles intereferes—Madame de Chatillon—The Cardinal leaves for France—Triumphant Return—Magistrates offer Homage—Absolute Submission 209

CHAPTER XXV
MAZARIN AGAIN IN POWER

Le Grand Spoliateur—Olympe Mancini—Marries Comte de Soissons—Madame Mancini—Marie Mancini—The King's Rudeness—Mazarin's Speech to the Envoy—Spanish Alliance 220

CHAPTER XXVI
A WIFE FOR LOUIS XIV

Princesse Marguerite of Savoy—Indignation of King of Spain—Louis is Stubborn—Anne in Despair—Peace and the Infanta—Departure of Princess of Savoy 229

CHAPTER XXVII
LOUIS XIV. AND MARIE MANCINI

Anne's Indignation with the Minister—The Cardinal remonstrates—The Lovers' Parting—Diplomatic Arrangements—End of Romance 236

CONTENTS

CHAPTER XXVIII
TREATY OF PEACE AND MARRIAGE OF LOUIS XIV

Marriage by Proxy—Spanish Wedding-dress—Meeting between Anne and Philip—Louis first sees Marie-Thérèse—Family Dinner-party—Royal Wedding—Queen-Mother returns to Paris 242

CHAPTER XXIX
DEATH OF MAZARIN

Betrothal of Monsieur—Hortense de Mancini—Cardinal's increasing Malady—The King's Grief—The Queen's Devotion Death of Mazarin 250

CHAPTER XXX
MAZARIN'S HEIRS

Lying-in-State—Abuse of the Dead Cardinal—His Enormous Wealth—His Personal Legacies—Death of Madame de Chevreuse 257

CHAPTER XXXI
CONCLUSION

Death of Anne—Lasting Love between Queen and Cardinal   263

LIST OF ILLUSTRATIONS

ANNE OF AUSTRIA. From the portrait in the Louvre (Photogravure) . . . . . . *Frontispiece*

                                                              Facing page

ANNE AT THE TIME OF HER MARRIAGE. After P. Marette, 1692 16

ANNE ON HORSEBACK. After F. David 38

ANNE AS A WIDOW. After Ph. Champigne 76

CARDINAL MAZARIN. From the engraving by F. Nanteuil (Photogravure) 100

MAZARIN IN HIS GALLERY. From an engraving by Nanteuil after Chauveau 128

QUEEN ANNE AND THE CARDINAL. From a sketch by R. P. Bonington 234

QUEEN AND CARDINAL

CHAPTER I

THE MARRIAGE OF LOUIS

ON a bright morning in late autumn in 1615 a long cavalcade of gentlemen, followed by soldiers bearing spears and pennants glistening in the sunlight, might have been seen descending the steep road leading down to the Spanish border, where the rushing waters of the Bidassoa flowed through the rich valley. This stream, which falls into an estuary at the south of the Bay of Biscay, has its name from a Basque word signifying "clearness," the waters being remarkable for their purity. The river had long been a subject of contest between France and Spain, forming as it does the boundary between the two countries; but in the fifteenth century Louis XII. and Ferdinand I. concluded an agreement by virtue of which the river became common to both nations.

The foremost riders among the cavalcade, shading

their eyes from the oblique rays of the winter sun, were looking anxiously to see whether on the opposite shore any advancing party was coming from the north.

In the midst of this goodly company was borne with due state a royal litter, adorned with the arms of Spain, the rich curtains of which being drawn aside a bright young face looked out, also anxiously scanning the distant scene.

A mere girl, almost a child, hardly suited for the pomp and ceremony with which she was being treated; and yet the crown of France, the greatest of the European countries, was about to be placed on her youthful head. This young Princess was Donna Anna, the Infanta of Spain, who, surrounded by her court, was travelling to the country so soon to become her own, to be presented to her future husband, King Louis XIII.

She was still full of curiosity and girlish amusement, and the mighty affairs of State counted for nothing as yet with the little bride, though doubtless she was not without many fears, though she bravely kept them to herself. Just now her mind was centred upon a meeting about to take place which naturally was of the most absorbing character for her.

Madame Elisabeth of France, daughter of Henri IV., the young sister of the juvenile King Louis XIII., was on her way to the court which Donna Anna had just left, to marry the Infante of Spain, afterwards Philippe IV. This exchange of brides, the result of many negotiations, held to be advisable for the peace of Europe, was about to take place.

The night before the Spanish court had halted at Fuenterrabia, a beautiful old town that rises like an amphitheatre on the side of a hill at the head of the Gulf of Gascony, near the left bank of the Bidassoa.

Philippe III., King of Spain, who accompanied his daughter, was closely allied to the House of Austria both by birth and marriage, and his only daughter had been given the name of his mother, "Anne of Austria," a name which she bore for the rest of her life—a proud title which even as Queen of France she would not forgo. Philippe adored his young daughter, and, though the match may have satisfied his ambitions, his heart was sore at the coming separation. It was a cruel one for him, and contrary to all etiquette he determined to remain with her to the very last moment; for this interchange was to take place in the centre of the river which was the boundary of the Spanish dominions.

As the party descended on their side of the river, they had come in sight of the preparations below, which were of a very curious nature, and the details of which have been preserved for us in the old records of the day.[1] At the narrowest passage of

[1] "L'Arrivée de la royne a Sainct Jean de LVS, 1615. L'ordres prescriptes des ceremonies, 1615. Par grace et permission il est permis a Sylvestre Moreau Marchant, libraire et colleporteur de faire imprimer, par tel Imprimerie que bon lui semblera les ceremonies faictes et obsernées a St. Jean de Lus a l'eschange des Infantes de France et d'Espagne. Et deffences a tous autres Imprimeurs et libraires de les imprimer ou contrefaire son permission."

the Bidassoa three rafts or boats had been prepared. On two of them had been erected royal pavilions, with crowns of France and Spain respectively on each of them. The pillars supporting them were draped with rich embroideries of gold and silver in beautiful designs. The expense was said to have been shared in common by the two countries; but there was no question that the preparations made by the Spaniards were far more grandiose, and the costliest materials and the most brilliant display of gold and silver were employed for their side of the passage.

Two of the barges were moored at the opposite sides of the stream, and it was decreed that the royal brides were to rest in their separate tents, while the whole of the baggage and suites of both parties crossed the river. Perhaps "tent" is hardly the proper word to use, though the pavilions were draped with curtains, for fear of bad weather had occasioned all preparations to be made against inconvenience from rain; and chimneys had been built, for the year was waning and, in spite of the bright southern sun, the weather was decidedly chilly.

The third barge in the centre, equally handsomely decorated, was not meant as a resting-place, but only as a passage from one country to the other.

To prevent confusion there were barriers fixed for some distance on either side of the river, to keep out the multitude, and to leave the roads clear for the royal cortèges.

The procession had halted on the mountain-side,

and, no one yet being in sight on the winding pass descending on the other side, a cry of dismay arose among the Spanish ranks.

Had the French failed in fulfilling their contract, thus offering an insult to the throne of Spain? If so, they would all be dishonoured as a nation. Donna Anna turned pale at the ominous sounds around her, and longed to clasp her father's hand, for protection and help; but he was riding ahead of her litter. It was a journey not without risk, and fears were entertained that the army of the Huguenots might oppose the entrance into France, even when the passage of the Bidassoa had been safely accomplished.

Then a shout arose from the soldiers, for a horseman had just appeared in sight, and soon a long train similar to their own, surrounding the litter of Madame Elisabeth, wound slowly down the winding road on the opposite shore.

Strict orders had been issued that, once in sight of each other, they were to travel at exactly the same pace, and reach the two shores at the same moment.[1] At a signal the litters were lowered and the curtains drawn aside, and the Princesses, in their royal robes, alighted in view of the vast crowd. The Duc de Guise escorted "Madame," and if the preparations of the French hardly equalled those of the Spaniards, he made up for this by the number of his followers. All the flower of the French army were ranged in battle array

[1] *L'Ordre Prescrites des Ceremonies*, MDC.XV.

behind them, with orders to wait and form the escort of the new Queen, while a band of violins, trumpets, and drums were ready to welcome her with a burst of music and herald her entrance into Bayonne. A lane was formed by the rival courtiers, and the brides walked through them to their separate pavilions, amid the rolling of the drums and the shouting of the people. Rest and refreshment were naturally much needed by the whole party, and they had ample leisure for it during the passage of the baggage and attendants, which took some time. Here, too, the farewells had to be said. Little " Madame's " adieux were of a formal nature, but Anna clung to her father and passionately embraced him. When all was ready, the signal was given; the two barges were slowly moved from the banks, till they reached the mutual ground in the middle of the stream. The orders were that the princesses should pass each other, giving a right hand, and that the gentlemen- and ladies-in-waiting should do the same, so that there might be no delay or confusion; those in charge had to see that these orders were carried out. But when the two little girls met (for Anna was only fifteen, and Elisabeth eleven) strict etiquette was set aside, and the new sisters warmly embraced, as they stood each on the border of their respective territories. Then Anna stepped on to the French barge, and as it slowly glided to the shore her Spanish life was over now she was Queen of France. Entering the litter of "Madame," she was borne through her welcoming subjects on the way to Bayonne.

The expectant bridegroom, King Louis XIII., was only a boy of fifteen, a few days younger than the Infanta. The negotiations for this marriage had been going on for years, and had begun before the tragic death of his father, Henri IV. At that time the young couple were children, not yet ten years old. Louis had been a sickly boy, and had been reared with difficulty by his *gouvernante*, Madame de Monglat. He needed constant care; but being always in the hands of his physicians, who were perpetually giving him medicines, he had little chance of being either manly or robust.[1] But though weak in body, his mind was even in those early days not without ambition, and he had a great idea of his own powers, and resented any interference from others. At his coronation, when the Prince de Condé, thinking the sceptre would be too heavy, interfered, to relieve him of his load, he turned to him angrily and exclaimed, "Non! non! je veux porter mon sceptre seul," a remark which has a melancholy interest when we remember how signally he failed to carry out even his own ideas of government. He was not without some accomplishments; he was fond of music and versifying, and had a great love of geography. When a small boy, he would make rose-leaves float in his bath, and call them "ships sailing from

---

[1] *Vie Particulière de Louis XIII.*, par Herouard, son premier Médecin.

India to Goa"; but his great passion was for birds. In appearance he was not bad-looking, but built on rather delicate lines.

This was the youth who was awaiting the arrival of Donna Anna of Spain. Not with much impatience, for he was very averse to the marriage, though his mother, Marie de' Medici, had done her best to encourage him, and to persuade him he might find other pleasures than that of the chase, to which he was devoted.

He was willing enough, however, to set off for Bordeaux with a train of soldiers to meet his bride. His physician, M. Herouard, writes in his journal of August 17: "The King awoke at 4.30, too impatient to start on his journey to delay even an hour. His face was bright and gay, and he was dressed with care. After an early breakfast he went booted and spurred to say his prayers in the Chapelle de Bourbon, and before seven o'clock the cortège had set out for Bordeaux."[1]

During the time he had to wait at that town for the arrival of the bride, he did not think it necessary to change his childish habits and occupations. He looked after his dogs and his birds, sometimes he assumed the dress of a *pantaleone* as a masquerade, or would make masse pans (or almond sweetmeat) for his delectation.[2] Occasionally the idea of the impending ceremony would overwhelm him, and he would spend the day in tears, and then forget his woes in hawking.

[1] *Journal de Herouard*, vol. 4.   [2] A. Baschet, *Le Roi chez la Reine*.

Primed by his advisers, he wrote a letter of welcome to meet Anna at Bayonne, whence a courier was to be despatched directly on her arrival, so that he might be in readiness for her. This letter has been preserved; but though it came from the royal pen, it is hard to say whether the sentiments were Louis' own, or dictated to him.[1]

"MADAME,

"Ne pouvant selon mon desir me trouver aupres de vous, a l'entrée de mon Royaume, pour vous mettre en possession du pouvoir que j'ai, comme aussi de mon entière affection, de vous aimer et servir, j'envoi Luines vers vous, un de mes plus confident serviteurs, pour en mon nom, vous saluer, et vous dire que vous êtes attendue de moi avec impatience, pour vous offrir moi-même l'un et l'autre. Je vous prie donc le recevoir favorablement, et le croire de ce qu'il vous dira de la part Madame, de votre plus amy et serviteur.

"LOUIS."

It was the Duc de Luynes who presented this letter from his royal master on Anna's arrival at Bordeaux, and accompanied her to the Bishop's Palace, which had been prepared for her reception, and he had orders to bring her by the same route that had been passed over by Madame Elisabeth

---

[1] This letter is part of a pamphlet which was printed at the time in Paris at the "Imprimerie Antoine du Brucil entre le Pont St. Michel, et la rue de la Harpe a l'etoile couronnée. M.D.C.XV., avec permission."

when on her way to Spain, the Duc de Guise being also in charge.

As the new Queen proceeded in her litter, she little knew that five miles from Bordeaux the King in disguise had mingled with the crowd that lined the road, in order that he might satisfy his boyish curiosity as to his bride.

Even in those early years she was tall, with a well-proportioned figure. Her eyes were very fine, combining in their depths both seriousness and gentleness, with a charm that in after-years proved fatal to more than one illustrious personage. She had magnificent hair of a chestnut colour in great waving masses, which she delighted in combing and dressing herself. She had the rare gift of beautiful hands, extremely white and perfect in shape ; they were soon the admiration of all Europe. On this occasion she was dressed in a petticoat of silver brocade, which showed between the folds of her green satin travelling habit, made with long, hanging sleeves. Round her neck was a diamond chain, the gift of Louis. A green velvet cap to match, with a black heron's plume at the side, was placed on her fair curls, and set off the rich colouring of her hair.[1]

As the cavalcade neared Bordeaux the salvos of the artillery and the roll of drums announced their arrival. The litter, by order, was thrown open so that all might behold their future Queen. At the palace, where she first halted, two state rooms had

[1] *Mémoires de Madame de Motteville*, vol. i.

been prepared, one for Louis and one for Anna. In that of the latter a daïs had been erected, covered with black velvet—a somewhat funereal throne for a bride.

Four days were granted to her before the final ceremony, that she might rest from her journey; but they were not spent, as she doubtless expected, with the young bridegroom at her side.

Every possible homage was offered to her by the court, but not even Marie de' Medicis could awake any enthusiasm in her son. To the disgust of every one, he went off duck-shooting the day after Anna's arrival, an act of neglect and disrespect that even the very youthful bride could not have failed to notice.

On Sunday they were obliged to attend mass together, the sulky boy and the timid girl, who were so soon to be bound by an irrevocable tie. But this was an act of religion, not of ceremony; they wore their ordinary dress, and were attended only by their immediate suite. This was Friday, the 29th, which must afterwards have been reckoned an unlucky day, for on the return of the Queen to her apartments they were startled by a loud noise, and a beam came crashing down beside the chimney-piece, where a moment before Anna had been standing warming her hands by the fire. Fortunately she had moved away, otherwise the accident must have proved fatal.[1] As it was, the room was filled with dust and débris, and the ladies shivered

[1] Le Gouven.

at the evil augury. Anna herself was considerably frightened; she realised what an escape she had had, and desired that a thanksgiving service should be held in the cathedral, which she attended, as did also a large concourse of people. No mention, however, is made of Louis having accompanied her.

The marriage took place on November 25, with all the state that attends the wedding of a sovereign. In spite of his former neglect, Louis was very attentive on the auspicious day, and looked his best in the white satin and violet velvet of his full dress. The young couple were curiously like each other; they seemed more like brother and sister, and such their relations continued to be for four years. Louis had no desire for any closer union, and on account of his extreme youth he was allowed to have his own way. He had been pampered and petted all his life, and we read of his nurse taking a prominent part in the arrangements. He had absolutely no idea of inconveniencing himself for any one; being fatigued after the ceremony, he retired at six o'clock to sup alone and go to bed.[1]

The journey of the royal pair to Paris was one long scene of rejoicing. An escort of 4,000 horse protected them on their way, and their arrival at the Louvre was conducted with great state. The new Queen, in a blaze of diamonds—even her dress sprinkled with precious stones—appeared on the

[1] A. Baschet, *Le Roi chez la Reine.*

balcony and threw largesse to the people, an amusement which suited the boyish Louis well. He entered into it with zest, and the days that followed were spent in fêtes and revelry.

But through it all the King took no part in matters of State and politics, and saw but little of his wife.

Anne, as she was now called,[1] filled every one with admiration at her modest and prudent behaviour. The grave and courtly manners she had acquired in Spain stood her in good stead at this trying moment. Her exalted but lonely position, and her extreme youth, called forth much pity from many of her subjects—indeed, a young girl could hardly have been placed in a more difficult position.

[1] Anne, a name borne by many celebrated women, was derived from the Hebrew word signifying "gracious."

CHAPTER II

THE INFATUATION OF BUCKINGHAM

VERY soon after the marriage the young Queen was deprived of her Spanish household, all her ladies being sent away except Donna Estefana, to whom she was tenderly attached. She was an elderly lady, who had had the charge of Anne in her childhood, and acted now as first bed-chamber woman. Anne's knowledge of French was still imperfect, so there was really a necessity for this lady's services being retained, otherwise the position of the new sovereign would have been one of real forlornness. Among her suite was a Spanish lady of a noble family in Madrid, who had married Monsieur Bertaud, one of the gentlemen-in-waiting at the French court.[1]

It was by order of Cardinal Richelieu that Anne was thus cut off as much as possible from communication with Spain; but he made an exception in favour of Madame Bertaud, who was useful as interpreter to the Queen. She not only remained for many years in her Majesty's confidence, but her place was afterwards filled by her daughter,

[1] *Mémoires de Madame de Motteville*, vol. i.

Madame de Motteville ; it is to her we are indebted for much information as to the private life of Anne of Austria, whose devoted companion she remained to the end of her life.[1]

Through the connivance of Mme. Bertaud the Queen was able to carry on a correspondence with her relatives at the court of Spain. This filled her with guilty joy, for she was not long in finding out that she was surrounded by enemies, whom she took pleasure in circumventing. Chief among them was the Duc de Luynes, to whom she had been specially consigned at the beginning of her married life, and who had the audacity to propose to Louis that it would be advisable to repudiate his wife, in order to marry a relation of the Duchesse de Luynes. When the Duchess heard this rumour she turned it into ridicule. She was filled with pity for the poor young Queen, and did her utmost to win her confidence and love ; but Anne turned away from her advances with disgust, so great had become her hatred and contempt for De Luynes, as she naturally concluded that the husband and wife were acting in concert. Desiring to please Louis, and also not wishing to be debarred from the hunting-parties and other amusements, she suffered herself to come in contact with De Luynes. This man had been a simple country gentleman of Avignon ; but his

[1] The earlier part of these memoirs is to be found in a manuscript in the Bibliothèque de l'Arsenal. The memoirs are not continued, however, later than 1644. The best edition of the whole work is that published in 1723.

knowledge of the habits of birds and his skill in taming them had endeared him to Louis, and he was put in charge, and made Grand Master of the Royal Aviaries.

His power over the King gradually increased, and he would brook no rivals. It was at his connivance that the Maréchal d'Ancre was assassinated, and all the murdered man's possessions were given to De Luynes. He was then by degrees created Maréchal, Duke, Peer, Constable, and Keeper of the Seals. He married the Princesse Marie de Rohan, and never got over his pleasure at being allied to such a noble house.[1]

So the first six years of the loveless marriage passed away; all the joys that it produced for Anne were the pleasures of her exalted position. The death of De Luynes in 1621 perhaps gave her a feeling that she was now secure from any evil influence acting upon Louis.

During those years she had overcome her former prejudice, and learnt to find a real friend in the Duchesse de Luynes, who entered into all her little sorrows, seeking to alleviate them in every way, besides sharing all court amusements with her. This lady, who afterwards became Duchesse de Chevreuse, was young and gay and laughter-loving, and she persuaded the Queen that for young hearts all should be joyous; she turned everything into fun, even matters of weight and seriousness.

But De Luynes' death did not bring peace into

[1] Bazin de Raucon, *Histoire du Règne de Louis XIII.*

After P. Marette, 1692

ANNE OF AUSTRIA AT THE TIME OF HER MARRIAGE.

the court circle, for Marie de' Medici having become reconciled to her son, it only widened the breach between the husband and wife. His mother wished to be absolute with Louis, and therefore encouraged the misunderstanding between the royal pair; besides, she would not give Anne credit for either goodness or intelligence.

That Anne was coquettish and frivolous there is no doubt; the eyes of many of the courtiers were turned with open admiration on the fair young queen. The Duc de Montmorency,[1] though he had long been under the thraldom of the beautiful Marquise de Sablé, was among the number. Anne did not concern herself much at his attentions, and laughed openly at the infatuation of the old Duc de Bellegarde. Indeed, his gallantries were a source of amusement to the whole court, including the King, who, in spite of his somewhat jealous nature, turned the whole thing into ridicule. Anne flirted with and smiled on them all, but her heart was quite untouched. Certainly Louis had never made it beat the faster; she was as indifferent to him as he was to her, only the natural sweetness of her disposition made her kind and considerate towards him.

In 1625 an alliance was about to take place between the thrones of France and England, for a marriage was proposed between Charles I. and Henrietta Maria, the youngest sister of King Louis. This gave great satisfaction to both nations, and

[1] Uncle of the great Condé.

Marie de' Medici, whose soul was filled with ambition, craved to see her daughter raised to the throne. King Charles's favourite and chief adviser, the Duke of Buckingham,[1] was sent over to Paris to carry out the negotiations, laden with presents for the young bride. Richelieu had been very averse to this nobleman being sent on such an errand, and persuaded Louis to refuse to receive him as ambassador, his character being such that he was considered "equally dangerous to nations, kings, and husbands."[2]

George Villiers, Duke of Buckingham, had been endowed by nature with beauty and charm; he was said to be the handsomest man of his day. His power over his royal master is well known. Charles could not move in any matter without the advice of his favourite; nor did the King ever dare to oppose his wishes.

A boaster, as well as a libertine, Buckingham used to declare that he had been the lover of three queens. Intriguing and crafty, he dominated two kings, and he has lived in history as a type of courtier-like levity and fascinating vice. This was the man who dared to cast his audacious eyes on the innocent Queen of France.[3]

In spite of the objections of Richelieu, King Charles refused to send any other ambassador, and the alliance being of too important a nature to be

[1] George Villiers, Duke of Buckingham, born in 1592, assassinated 1628.
[2] *Mémoires de Richelieu*
[3] *Mémoires de Retz*, v. 4, p. 186.

abandoned on account of a prejudice, Buckingham was eventually received by Louis. He was entertained with all ceremony, in the presence of the two Queens and Princess Henrietta Maria. Anne's attention was attracted by the handsome envoy, whose grace of mind and body captivated her at once.

This was the beginning of that fatal episode in her life which somewhat unjustly brought down upon her the censure of her subjects, and for ever tarnished her fair fame.

As to Buckingham, feminine charms always inflamed his facile nature, and in describing the scene to his royal master he wrote of Anne and the bride-elect "as the two most perfect creatures in the world."

Buckingham was rich, magnificent, and liberal, as befitted the favourite of a great king; he had the spending of the royal treasures, and was decked with the royal jewels. He was generous, too, and of a sympathetic nature, but where women were concerned absolutely destitute of principle.

Anne was aware of his penetrating eyes fixed upon her as he gracefully carried out his high mission before the King, nor did he confine his admiration to glances only.[1] At the royal banquet he sat beside the Queen, and charmed her with his gallant bearing and flattering tongue. The embassy was to last only a week, but Buckingham lost no time. Under cover of the music at the State concert, he drew from Anne the avowal that if

[1] Cardinal de Richelieu, *Mémoires*.

she could admit a love for another rather than her husband it would be George Villiers who would be that favoured person.[1] Through it all Anne thought no harm nor intended any. She was not in love with Louis, so she made no secret of her admiration for Buckingham, and spoke openly of his many attractions of mind and body. It was the habit of her court, and of her day, to admit and be proud of a conquest. At her palace in Madrid she had been used to hear her Spanish ladies, who lived like cloistered nuns, and never spoke to a man in the presence of their King and Queen, boast of their love affairs, which, far from detracting from their reputations, seemed to enhance them.

The Duchesse de Chevreuse, now in constant attendance on the Queen, spent her whole life in intrigues, and Anne, in spite of the purity of her mind, must through the counsels of her friend have learnt to treat passion lightly, and seek to inspire it in the hearts of men, feeling all the time that her own virtue was unassailable. The time of revelry drew to a close. Anne, doubtless anxious to prolong it, announced her intention of accompanying her young sister-in-law as far as possible on the journey to England.

The court halted at Amiens on the way, and an incident that occurred there gave rise to much scandal. There was a very fine garden at the house where the royal ladies lodged, which for some reason was always kept locked, by order of

[1] *Mémoires de Motteville*, v. 1.

the King. Anne's curiosity was aroused, and as there was a great deal of difficulty in getting the key, she became still more desirous of entering it. It was somewhat late in the evening by the time the captain of the guard had thrown the gates open at her disposal, and she passed through them, accompanied by Madame de Chevreuse and some of her suite, among others the Duke of Buckingham.

The party strolled along the main avenue, and by degrees they scattered in different directions, and the Duke drew Anne into the dusk of one of the side alleys. Deep in conversation for a moment or two, the Queen did not notice that they were separated from the rest of the party, when suddenly Buckingham clasped her in his arms, making a passionate avowal of his love.

Terrified at his too ardent caresses, Anne gave a cry, and called loudly to her equerry. This very cry, which showed the innocence of her purpose, proved her undoing; the members of her suite rushed to her assistance and the affair could no longer be kept secret, and it was not long before it reached the ears of the King, as well as the whole court, where the story did not lose in the telling. The journey was resumed the following day to Calais, where they halted, and here Anne insisted on having a ball.

While treading a stately measure Buckingham doubtless found time to pour into the Queen's indulgent ears regret for the past and promise of prudence in the future, all the while that his eyes searched the very depths of hers; his prayer for pardon was more of a challenge than a petition. He had no intention of hurrying his departure, and let it be understood that the delay was in consequence of the Queen-Mother's indisposition. The experienced courtiers saw through these manœuvres, though possibly the Queen did not.

"La manière d'agir de cet étranger me déplaît beaucoup," writes the Comte de Brienne in his memoirs.[1] At last, even Buckingham could find no further pretext to delay—Charles was waiting impatiently for his bride—and he had to proceed with Henrietta Maria to England.

Anne, having taken leave of her sister-in-law, entered the royal carriage, and the Duke, bowing low, with his plumed hat in his hand, advanced bareheaded to make his adieux.[2]

He lifted the hem of her robe in courtly fashion to imprint a kiss upon it. The Princesse de Conté, who was sitting beside her royal mistress, discreetly looked the other way. Anne's ladies were fond of her, and sympathised, not always wisely, with her; some may have aided her little follies maliciously, pleased to see her descending from her pedestal above their heads; so Buckingham stood unheeded. Holding the curtain which hung over the window of the coach, he drew it forward as a screen, and

---

[1] *Mémoires du Comte de Brienne.*
[2] *Mémoires de Motteville.*

with tears rolling down his cheeks murmured some broken words of farewell; while Anne, bending forward, her fine eyes full of tears, forgiving all his audacity, strove to mitigate his grief at his departure.

Doubtless she thought this was a last good-bye, but her crafty lover intended otherwise. Perhaps it was more passion than craft, for George Villiers was of a susceptible, amorous nature. Anyway, instead of crossing the Channel immediately he pretended he had received important communications from his sovereign, which rendered it necessary for him to return once more to Paris, to confer with the Queen-Mother.

Leaving the Princess at the seashore, he started back to discuss a perfectly imaginary negotiation; but arriving early at the Louvre he repaired at once to Anne's apartments, and, having forced his way into her chamber, found her still in bed. Falling on his knees beside her, he kissed the sheets with ardour, while inarticulate sobs broke from him as he bent his handsome head in an attitude of despair on the lace draperies of the bed.

Anne remained frozen in silent dismay, perhaps even fear, and a painful silence ensued.

Then the whole awkwardness and impropriety of the Duke's conduct caused her ladies to feel it was their duty to interfere, and the old Comtesse de Lannoi, who stood at the head of the bed, told Buckingham with great severity that such manners were not in vogue in France, and attempted to make him rise from his kneeling position. But he, resisting her efforts, told her that he was not a Frenchman, and that he was not obliged to observe the rules of that country; then turning once more to the Queen, he loaded her with terms of endearment. But by this time Anne had become mistress of herself; she reproached him for his temerity, and—in a voice from which, however, all anger was absent—calmly told him to leave her presence.

With one long adoring look, Buckingham slowly rose to his feet and obeyed his lady's order. Nothing, however, could daunt this ardent lover. The following day he had the audacity to approach the Queen again, in the sight of Marie de' Medici and the whole court, and made his formal and last adieux, fully determined in his own mind, however, to return before long.

The King was at Fontainebleau, so, as soon as the English ambassador had withdrawn, the two queens left the Louvre to join him. Thus this early romance of Anne's life was at an end, but not the consequences of it. The whole affair had been brought forward too publicly to be lightly passed over. The careless equerry was dismissed, as were others of the suite.[1] Everything to the disadvantage of the Duke of Buckingham was poured into Anne's ears, but she only held her proud head the higher, and with compressed lips listened in unbelieving silence. She had meant no wrong, and she had done no wrong, and she would

[1] *Mémoires de la Porte.*

not allow herself to be browbeaten in this fashion; before her eyes she still saw the handsome face of her English lover, and in her ears she still heard the alluring tones of his voice.

But she never saw Buckingham again. When the following year Henrietta Maria was anxious to return to see her mother, she tried to persuade Charles to let her travel to France under the charge of Buckingham. But both Louis and his mother absolutely refused to receive him; aided in this matter by the Cardinal Richelieu, they remained firm, and George Villiers was never able to re-visit France. Madame de Chevreuse mischievously kept the flame alight by forever talking of him to Anne. The Queen and her favourite hated Richelieu, whom they looked on as the originator of all their annoyances; it was their chief pleasure to thwart him, all the more so that Anne was persuaded that he insinuated many things into the King's ear.

In after-years she saw how the light-heartedness of youth had led her blindly into grievous error, and it was owing to the Duchesse de Chevreuse that she had acted with such want of judgment. But wherever the fault might have lain, this affair with Buckingham proved fatal to the young Queen's future, for it was never forgotten, or forgiven, by either the King or his people.

CHAPTER III

RICHELIEU INTERVENES

A FAR worse adventure befell Anne the following year. She made the discovery, when travelling to Nantes, that the Queen-Mother, Marie de' Medici, and Cardinal Richelieu were working together to have her sent back in disgrace to Spain.

This treatment, which she had long dreaded, was more than the unhappy Queen could endure in silence. In one matter she did indeed confess that she had been acting in a manner not free from intrigue. She had been doing her best to prevent the marriage of Monsieur the King's brother and heir with Mademoiselle de Montpensier.

The astrologers had declared that Louis would not live very long, and to increase the popularity of their predictions they accused the Queen of a desire to marry her brother-in-law after her husband's death. This was the pretext for the animosity now displayed towards Anne. She admitted that she had dreaded the idea of the marriage of Monsieur, as long as she remained childless; for should an heir be born of any such union, she feared lest the Queen-Mother should attempt to have her repudiated. The charge now brought against her was, however, of far more grave meaning than merely any foolish wishes she might have expressed on her somewhat feeble attempts at opposition to those far stronger than herself. It was no less than a distinct accusation of a very grave nature.

It was a love intrigue in the first instance that provoked the trouble.[1]

M. de Jouvigni was madly in love with Madame de Chevreuse. That fair disturber of the public peace, while possessing all the qualities suitable for political intrigue, was "feminine" in the highest degree; in this lay at once her strength and her weakness.

De Jouvigni, full of jealousy, and swayed by the passions which ambition and desire provoke, made an accusation against the Marquis de Chalais, whom he suspected of being the Duchess's lover, of having made an attempt on the King's life.

De Chalais eagerly repudiated the idea; in company with others he certainly had helped to prevent the marriage of Monsieur with Madame de Montpensier, on the plea that it was better for all parties that a foreign princess should be chosen; and owing to his passionate love for Madame de Chevreuse he had doubtless worked with more ardour than discretion, knowing that she also had this cause at heart; but treachery to his sovereign was very far from his thoughts.[2]

---

[1] *Mémoires de Motteville.*
[2] Henri de Talleyrand, Marquis de Chalais, was born in 1599, and executed in 1627.

But he had incurred the ill-will of Richelieu, who, in order to increase his power over the King, had persuaded him that his throne and his life were threatened by a number of noblemen who had formed a cabal against him, and he further inflamed his master by making him believe that the Queen was implicated in this plot.

Even the cold-blooded Louis received this intelligence with doubt and dismay, and refused to listen to such a charge. But Richelieu knew of means by which he could press it further home. He repaired to the prison where the Marquis lay under sentence of death, and assured him of a free pardon if he would swear that the Queen was also in the plot. The wretched man, in a moment of fear and weakness, with the stern Minister standing over him, thinking that the King would never believe aught against his wife, gave the desired information, and Richelieu, hastening back to the royal presence, amplified the reluctant words he had dragged from his prisoner, and so persuaded the King that the statement was true.

Horrified at learning that instead of a faithful wife he had a murderess ever beside him, the unhappy Louis was in a state bordering on frenzy; he sent for Anne to attend the council, and there before all denounced her as having conspired against his life, for the sake of having another husband.[1]

The Queen, magnificent in her rich attire, stood

[1] *Mémoires de Motteville*, vol. i.

before him in all her beauty, and looked at him out of her calm eyes, with their steadfast glance. Bravely she forced back the tears of natural indignation that welled within them, for she was supported by the knowledge of her own innocence. Outraged as she was in her tenderest feelings as a woman and a wife, in a firm voice she replied to the charge, generously withholding all anger and animosity towards the King.

She declared her absolute innocence of such a crime; turning towards her mother-in-law, who stood beside the King, she reproached her bitterly for this last persecution intended to bring about her ruin.

As Anne of Austria, the proud Infanta of Spain, she looked her accusers in the face without faltering, and then asked permission to withdraw.[1] But it is ever hard to persuade others of an untruth when their wish is to think evil, and she might never have been cleared of this charge had not the perfidy of Richelieu defeated its own ends. Though he had promised a pardon to the Marquis de Chalais, he took no further steps in the matter. Perhaps he feared further revelations should the prisoner be set at liberty. From the day that he had falsely accused the Queen, De Chalais had never had a moment's peace, though he had fully determined to repair the evil some day. But when his accusers came to lead him out to execution

---

[1] Louis said of his wife, "Dans l'état où je suis je dois lui pardonner, mais je ne suis pas obligé de la croire."—*Mémoires de la Rochefoucauld.*

he saw that he had been fooled and forsaken by the Minister.

He sent his confessor at once to the King to tell him the whole truth, and told him also to go and implore pardon of Anne for having been persuaded under the fear of death and by false promises to accuse her of treachery towards the Sovereign.

Not only did these words of a condemned man on the scaffold carry weight, but his mother the Marquise de Chalais sought an audience with the Queen, and her description was so vivid and graphic that it left no doubt in the minds of her hearers as to the truth of her story.

Her unhappy son's knowledge of the Queen's jealous dislike of the marriage had been turned into a weapon against him, and his fatal weakness had been his ruin. All that came of this incident was increased fear and hatred on the part of Anne towards Richelieu. In spite of opposition, Monsieur finally married Mademoiselle de Montpensier, a marriage which after all brought a great deal of happiness into Anne's life, for she learned to love her sister-in-law in the years to come ; Richelieu's vengeance, however, took the form of procuring the dismissal from court of the Duchesse de Chevreuse, which was a great blow to Anne, who was very fond of her, and knew not how to live without her society, but in reality it was a fortunate occurrence.

Madame de Chevreuse had been the Queen's evil genius all through. A woman so entirely occupied with vanity and intrigue was no fit companion to a young princess who was still in ignorance of all the dangers that surrounded her. That very ignorance made her unconscious of the advantages that accrued from the departure of the Duchess, but Anne's bitterness was increased against Richelieu, whom she credited with having destroyed the peace of her existence.

Still, we cannot be surprised that the Queen suffered at being parted from her friend, who was a woman of no ordinary talent. Her moral sense was indeed deficient; it was well known that she had many lovers, and she used to say herself that by "a strange caprice she never loved most the one she esteemed most."[1] For the attraction of the moment she would go any lengths, brave any perils, but the slightest distraction would turn her attention to a fresh object.

In spite of the assertions of Cardinal Retz, it is doubtful whether Buckingham had ever been the Duchess's lover, though possibly she did always speak of him as "ce pauvre Buckingham," nor can we altogether credit the celebrated picture which the Cardinal drew of her in his *Mémoires*.[2] It was *outré* and extravagant, as were many of his descriptions. The Marquis de Chalais had undoubtedly been one of her lovers, and when she saw his tragic end on the scaffold she was transported with rage as well as with grief. After this lamentable affair Richelieu, who had failed altogether to win her over to his side,

---

[1] *Mémoires de Motteville.*
[2] *Mémoires de Cardinal de Retz*, v. 3, p. 104.

declared she did more harm than any other person; certainly to be planning and plotting was the breath of her nostrils. Sure of obtaining help from the Duke of Buckingham and Lord Holland (another of her devoted admirers), she requested permission, if she had to leave court, to retire to England. But this the Cardinal would not allow, and she was obliged to go to Lorraine to a property of her own, which had been left her by her first husband. There she lived for intrigue, and tried to form a European league with England and Austria, with the help of Charles IV. of Lorraine.[1] She found a willing abettor in the Duke of Buckingham. His vanity, as well as his affections, was sorely hurt by the episode at the Court of France, and his ambition was equally checked. He was glad to provoke a war between the two countries, and in a letter to Lord Holland he made no secret of the true state of his feelings; when Louis arrived in July 1627 with his army and laid siege to La Rochelle, where the Huguenot rising had taken place, Buckingham arrived with a large naval force to their defence, openly showing his revenge, thus publicly proclaiming the passion for Anne in which he gloried.

But his pride was punished by the reverses he encountered.

Richelieu displayed almost superhuman activity.

[1] This man, Charles IV. of Lorraine and Duc de Guise, was a schemer who sided with whatever party and country paid the largest sum for permission to travel through his domain, which was the easiest route to Flanders (D'Haussonville).

He had made great preparations, both naval and military, and repaired to La Rochelle in company with the King. The Duke's design was on the Ile de Rhé, contrary to the advice he had been given, which was to land his men at the Ile d'Oleron, where the garrison was weak and the island ill provided, whereas Rhé was strongly fortified, and well furnished with necessaries.

His repulse followed on his ill-judged venture, and he abandoned the siege in disgust, and set sail for England.

This was the first time that the English, who used to bring glory from France, were repulsed with shame, and they did not soon recover the honour lost in this unhappy enterprise.

None the less Buckingham was received in England with all honour, as if he were a conquering victor. A second relief of La Rochelle was resolved on at court, and the Duke, to ingratiate himself with the people, undertook it with hopes of better success than at the Ile de Rhé.[1] These hopes were frustrated, for while superintending the preparations at Portsmouth he fell by the knife of the assassin Fenton, August 23, 1628.

As to Anne, had any love, even friendship, existed between her and Louis, and had she been able to speak openly to him, the uprightness of her thoughts might have caused him to forgive the follies of her youth.

[1] *Memoirs of the Life of George Villiers, 1st Duke of Buckingham.* Tract printed and sold by George Smeeton, 1819.

Louis had many good qualities, and being himself, lacked prudence, and also the co sense which an older man would have disp So if he was unkind to his wife he must n judged too harshly. Such a union as theirs hardly be productive of happiness.

CHAPTER IV

THE QUEEN AND THE COURT

WHILE the events just recorded point to the bad feeling between the Minister and the Queen, it is necessary to mention an idea very prevalent, which was that Richelieu felt more love than hate for the royal lady; and finding he could make no impression on her, he sought out of vengeance to injure her in the eyes of the King.[1]

No one had noticed his attentions or thought anything about them till these persecutions began, which lasted till the end of his life, but that Anne was conscious of them is certain. One day, finding himself alone with her, he burst into an impassioned address, and declared the burning love he felt for her. She was just about to rebuke him haughtily, and had turned a glance of withering scorn on him, when Louis entered the room and prevented her from speaking. The fitting opportunity being lost, she never chose to reopen the subject, not wishing the Cardinal to think that she considered

---

[1] A little work was published at Cologne in 1692 called *Les Amours d'Anne d'Autriche avec le Cardinal Richelieu*, which confirms this view.

his mad words of sufficient importance even to be remembered.

She only showed her consciousness of them by the contempt and hatred she could not conceal, and continued to refuse his advances and offers of friendship. Those about her, who did not love him either, helped to strengthen her feelings of aversion. Almost the whole court shared her sentiments, for all hated Richelieu. And there is no doubt that this open dislike displayed on all sides greatly increased Louis' aversion for his wife, he being so completely under the rule of his Minister.

The real monarch of France was Richelieu, and his reign was by no means a bad one for the country. The evil reports spread abroad about him by the enemies of the State were proof that he did not pander to their wishes, and at all events served his Sovereign.

Tormented by all these false accusations and unpleasantnesses, Anne began to weary of court life, and longed for some safe place where she might find peace; and thinking that no fault could be found with such a pious wish as to build an abbey, she bought a piece of ground in the outskirts of Paris and laid the first stone herself.[1] It was called " Val-de-Grace," or sometimes " Le Val Profond," and La Mère d'Arbouze, a friend of the Queen, was chosen as abbess.

But even in this sacred retreat poor Anne was allowed no peace. By Richelieu's advice the King

[1] *Mémoires de Motteville*, vol. i.

one day sent the Archbishop of Paris with orders to search the convent to see if any incriminating letters between the Queen and her brother, the King of Spain, might be found there. The frightened nuns ran hither and thither from cell to cloister, not knowing what fate was in store for them, till the Archbishop sternly ordered them to assemble in the great hall, and threatened them with excommunication should they speak one to another. Then he demanded the keys to be brought, and personally searched every cell, including the one set apart for the Queen, in the hopes of finding the incriminating papers.

None were, however, to be discovered, and all they saw were articles of discipline, such as hair shirts and belts studded with nails, so that the Chancellor Sequier, who accompanied the Archbishop, exclaimed: " Alas! we have found exactly the opposite of that which we were searching for." [1]

All that they carried away and handed to Richelieu was a closed casket in the Queen's cell, which on being opened was found to contain English gloves, a present from Henrietta Maria. This domiciliary visit ever remained a painful memory in Anne's mind, and she could never speak of it without tears.

The French court at that time was filled with lovely women. The Duchesse de Chevreuse and the Duchesse de Montbazon were among those

[1] *Mémoires de Motteville*, vol. i.

the fame of whose charms was noised abroad. The latter was a great beauty, tall and elegant; she was noticed wherever she moved, her stately figure superior among the rest; but her mind was not equal to her exquisite form. Her intelligence was limited, she was absolutely without talent, and could boast of one thing only—the number of her lovers. She and her beautiful daughter-in-law, the Princesse de Guémenée, used to dispute together as to which of them had the greater number of gallants. There was not much virtue or morality about the court of Louis XIII. But if the charms of these frail beauties were becoming somewhat *passés*, there were younger if less fair sirens about the palace: the Princesse Marie de Gonzague, afterwards the wearer of a royal crown; the handsome Mademoiselle de Rohan, whose pride was unequalled and whose virtue was unassailable; Mademoiselles de Guise, d'Hauteville, de Vendôme, and many others who gathered round Anne, formed a galaxy of loveliness at the fêtes at the Louvre, till the court at Paris became the envy of all other nations.

Pre-eminent among them all was Anne of Austria—that is, if we may believe her faithful bed-chamber woman, Madame de Motteville, whose pen never wearied of writing of the charms of mind and body of her adored mistress. The Queen at that time had reached the zenith of her beauty. She wore her hair much curled and often powdered, but at times she allowed the beautiful locks to fall

After F. David.

ANNE OF AUSTRIA.

in ringlets of their natural colour in great luxuriance. Her skin was very white, but she spoilt the effect by wearing too much rouge, a fashion she had brought from Spain. Her hazel eyes were clear and limpid, and her mouth was small. Her lips were those of the House of Austria, which gave her a distinction apart from, and superior to, women of otherwise great beauty. Her figure and height completed the regal air which caused all eyes to be turned upon her. Later, the stoutness that we see in her portraits took away from this queenly beauty.

Brilliant balls and State banquets succeeded each other, and on the surface all was bright and gay. The dark side of the picture lay in the person of Cardinal Richelieu, who worked in secret for the ruin of all those who stood in the way of his ambitions. From the first he had intrigued against the Queen-Mother and Anne. Marie de' Medici, who had contributed to the elevation of the Cardinal in the first instance, thought he was completely at her feet and ready to do her bidding, but on his failing once to carry out her wishes, she found that he had neither gratitude nor willingness to serve her, and her former liking turned to bitterest hate.[1] And this common dislike drew the two Queens together. After years of friction they suddenly formed a friendship; perhaps Marie de' Medici had some compunction for the part she had

---

[1] *Journal de Richelieu, dans les Archives curieuses de l'Histoire de France*, tome v.

played. She was, moreover, not without uneasiness. In her endeavours to get the upper hand, she had come into angry contact with the Minister, and had found that she had quite overrated her strength. She lived in hourly fear of being arrested, and turned in this extremity to the young Queen, who, not being of a revengeful nature, was more than ready to hold out the hand of fellowship.

CHAPTER V

THE "COUP DE COMPIÈGNE"

THE two Queens had gone to Compiègne together in January, 1631, and were holding the court there, the King having remained in Paris. A round of amusement was at once commenced, and carried on with much zest. After an evening spent in dance and song Anne was awakened from a sound sleep at a very early hour the following morning by some one knocking at her door; she called to her women to know if it was by any chance the King, he being the only one who could thus summon her in this familiar fashion.[1] She had thrown aside the curtains of her bed, and saw that the light was still faint, so she knew the hour was very early, and her mind was filled with alarm. An unknown terror pervaded her. What could the King's presence at such an untoward time mean but a menace against her person, or perhaps the order for her exile. Gathering all her failing courage, she prepared herself to receive the blow, whatever it might be. "Open the door," she said to her trembling women in a firm voice, for whatever her faults, Anne was

[1] *Mémoires de Motteville*, vol. i.

no coward, nor did she flinch when she saw who it was that craved admittance—for it was the Keeper of the King's Seals, and his presence seemed but to confirm her fears.

The bedroom of royalty in those days appears to have been open to all comers, and the idea that it was intrusion on a lady's privacy did not seem to occur to any of them.

The King's ambassador, bowing low, approached the bedside, and informed Anne that it was his royal master's pleasure that the Queen-Mother should be considered under arrest, and that it was his desire that his wife should hold no communication with the disgraced Queen, but that she should repair without loss of time to the Church of the Capucines, where he intended to meet her.

It was a strange scene: the half-darkened chamber, the hastily lighted taper that one of the women was holding, throwing dark shadows among the rich hangings of the couch, blended with the faint light of the coming dawn seen through the open casement. The ambassador, booted and spurred and travel-stained, looked from the scared white faces of the ladies to the fair young Queen, who, seated erect under the crimson canopy of her bed, with dishevelled hair, listened with a calm countenance, on which, however, intense surprise was depicted, to the orders of her husband the King.

She simply bowed her acknowledgments of these orders, and, requesting the withdrawal of the royal messenger, proceeded to rise with all haste. Not, however, with the idea of obeying them, for she determined to hasten at once to her mother-in-law's room. Only half attired, with a morning robe thrown over her nightdress, and with hair unbound, Anne ran down the private corridor and tapped gently at the door.

"It is I—Anne," she exclaimed; "let me come in," as she turned the handle and entered.

The Queen-Mother, who had also been startled out of her sleep by the unusual noises, was sitting up in bed, crouched in an attitude of fear, with her hands clasped round her knees.

"Oh, my daughter," she cried. "Am I to be murdered, or made a prisoner? What is the King's good pleasure?"

The Queen, filled with compassion, threw herself into the arms of the elder woman, folding her in a warm embrace, and, forgetting all the insults that Marie de' Medici had at one time heaped upon her, mingled her tears with those of her disgraced mother.

These royal ladies knew well that they were the victims of Richelieu's malice, who was the enemy of both alike; but they did not realise that that embrace was to be their last. When Anne had hurriedly told her tale she begged leave to withdraw, as she had to make the necessary toilet to join the King as she had been directed to do.

When left alone the Queen-Mother faced the situation. She was terrified at the idea of the prison at Compiègne, at the same time she was anxious not to implicate her daughter-in-law, whom she had at last learnt to love very dearly. Nothing was left for her but flight, and this she determined to effect without loss of time.

With all haste she made her preparations, calling her women about her; and without state or suite, without jewels, or even the necessaries of life; the proud Marie de' Medici, once all-powerful, in disguise, and accompanied only by her women, fled by a back door and mounting into a common hired vehicle was within a few hours wending her way towards the frontier; while Anne, who had obediently set off to the Capucines to meet the King, was quite unaware of what was going on in the palace in her absence, and not daring to risk Louis' displeasure, she returned to Paris with him still in ignorance of the flight of the old Queen.[1] This was called the "Coup de Compiègne," and it was said that the whole thing was a ruse on the part of Richelieu, who wished to remove Marie de' Medici out of his way.[2] Be this as it may, the King knew well that the nation at large blamed him greatly for his most unfilial conduct, and the severity that was meted out by his orders to his mother's adherents also called forth much indignation.

Anxious to propitiate his people, he treated his wife somewhat better, and saw her more often, and as she was greatly beloved, this gave much satisfaction.

---

[1] Marie de' Medici reached Flanders in safety. She wandered about for some years, and at last died, overcome by misery and sorrow, at Cologne in 1642.

[2] *Mémoires de la Porte.*

Richelieu also saw fit to curry favour with the Queen by recalling the Duchesse de Chevreuse from her exile in Lorraine. No doubt the wily lady promised the Cardinal to do everything that he wished; perhaps he was not insensible to her personal charms. She was only thirty, and in the height of her beauty. The Queen loved her, and could not do without her, and for that reason Madame de Chevreuse had lost the good graces of the Minister, as he was bent on preventing any intimacies that interfered with his plans, but it suited his policy of the moment to bring her back.

Happy in the society of her friend, Anne, who was young and sanguine, re-entered upon her life with fresh zest. She cast behind her the troubles and worries of the past, and, forgetting even her enemy Richelieu, passed her time in diversion and mirth. One desire of her heart, however, remained ungratified, and that was to become the mother of a Dauphin; this indeed was the earnest wish of the whole country.

But if on the surface all was calm, the Minister was working none the less against the Queen. All the futile cabals of which she had been guilty were made known at once to Richelieu by his spies, although for various reasons he gave no sign of having discovered the Queen's many political intrigues with her Spanish relations.

In 1633 François de Rochechouart, Chevalier de Jars, who had fallen under the ban of the Cardinal's displeasure, was recalled from his exile in England, where he had been sent on account of his attachment to the Queen.

Richelieu, who looked upon him as one of the chief conspirators, finding that he was spending the period of his disgrace very agreeably, had him recalled. Chateauneuf, Keeper of the Seals and lover of the fair Chevreuse, was implicated as well, and the Cardinal was determined on the downfall of them both. The Duchess was once more exiled from court, but only as far as her Château de Dampierre. It was not very distant from the capital, and often at dusk she would come disguised as a man to Paris, and meet the Queen either at the Louvre or at the convent of Val-de-Grace, where the good sisters were ever ready to aid and abet her. The pleasure of the meeting was doubled by the risk they ran, and the adventurous Duchess would return after midnight to Dampierre, riding through the night with only one trusty servant. Needless to say, these visits were discovered, and she was ordered back to Touraine. The punishment was a severe one to the lovely Duchess, who was at an age when she might naturally wish for amusement. Buried in the country, far from Paris, politics, and intrigue, the only entertainment she could find was turning the head of the old Archbishop of Tours, and when this diversion began to pall she encouraged the visits of the young and amiable Comte de la Rochefoucauld.[1] For four long years, till 1637, this life went on, and all the time she kept up an

[1] *Memoires de la Rochefoucauld*, p. 335.

active correspondence with the Queen, Henrietta Maria, the Queen of Spain, and Charles of Lorraine, till even that seasoned adventurer fell a victim to her charms. The Queen wrote most of her letters at Val-de-Grace, and her confidential valet, La Porte, carried them back and forward, and to his memoirs we are indebted for these details of the Queen's private life.[1]

Meanwhile her fellow-culprit, the Chevalier de Jars, was having a far worse fate. He too was accused of complicity with the enemies of the King. He was arrested and sent to the Bastille, where he was kept in a dark cell for eleven months. It was in winter that this happened, and the black velvet coat he was wearing at the time remained on his person without being taken off during the whole of his incarceration.[2] He was led out to be interrogated eighty times, and he always replied to the charges brought against him with firmness and wisdom, never allowing himself to be implicated on any point, nor in any way endangering the safety of others.

One day he was suddenly removed by a guard, with all the appearance of being about to be taken to execution; and as they were going down the steps at the main entrance he saw a group consisting of the Maréchal de Bassompierre, the Marquis de Vieuville, Vautier, the late physician of Marie de' Medici, and others who were prisoners, but who had been

---

[1] *Mémoires de la Porte.*
[2] *Ibid.*

more humanely treated than himself. De Jars knew not what might be in store for him. Turning towards them he exclaimed, "Gentlemen, adieu. I know not whither I go. Rest assured whatever may be my fate I am a man of honour, and will never fail towards either my friends or myself, or betray either."[1]

He was taken to Troyes, where he was brought before the judge Laffemas, who had already tormented him at the Bastille, and who was commonly known by the title of "Hangman to the Cardinal."

A number of judges much of the same calibre formed a court, and they sought, by the means only such men knew how to employ, to make the Chevalier de Jars incriminate himself or others. They tried to bribe false witnesses, but one of their number, the Prevôt de l'Ile, who had accompanied De Jars from Paris, declined to be a party to any such manœuvre.

Laffemas knew well the wishes of Richelieu, which were not to take the life of the Chevalier, being too sure of his innocence to risk such a proceeding, and having, moreover, no proof by which he could bring about his condemnation. But he wished to work upon his fears by the apparent certainty of death, that he might be induced to give up the secret of the Queen's intrigue, that of Madame de Chevreuse, and of Chateauneuf, Keeper of the Seals, who was also implicated.

[1] *Mémoires de Motteville.*

Laffemas had promised Richelieu that he would so torment his victim that he would by degrees draw out of him enough to suit their purpose, and he so interrogated and threatened the Chevalier that, had he had a different sort of victim, he might have succeeded in his endeavours.

On All Saints' Day this treacherous judge, wishing to appear kindly disposed towards his prisoner, allowed him to attend mass; for this purpose a band of archers and the guard of the town escorted him to church. At the steps of the altar the Chevalier perceived Laffemas with his wife receiving the Holy Sacrament. He was the chief man of the province, but far more feared than liked. De Jars was a man of a passionate nature, and absolutely without fear, and, seeing this man in the act of receiving the chief blessing of the Church, he tore himself loose from his guards, and throwing himself upon Laffemas seized him by the throat, exclaiming:

"Traitor! With the Creator that you worship on your lips, now is the moment to tell the truth, and to justify me before God and man. Avow my innocence, or else be known of all men as a villain."[1]

At this outcry the people gathered round them; some shrugged their shoulders, but most murmured against this unjust judge.

The Prevôt de l'Ile tried to separate the two men, who still struggled together, but the Chevalier

[1] *Mémoires de Motteville*, vol. i.

de Jars would not let go his man, and still pressed for an answer.

When Laffemas at last could speak he replied coldly :

" Monsieur, you have nothing to complain of; the Cardinal loves you well."

He further added that De Jars would be probably released and sent to Italy, but that some of his own letters in their possession might prove his guilt.

The Chevalier did not understand what they were driving at, and thought himself lost. He was brought once more before the tribunal, and defended himself with such courage that he confounded those who sought to implicate his friends. As he was leaving the court the Prevôt de l'Ile approached him and said·

" Monsieur, be of good courage, I have hopes for you. My orders are to bring you back to the same prison, while if a man is condemned he is generally taken elsewhere."

The Chevalier replied:

" I thank you, my friend, for your encouraging words, but those rascals intend to condemn me ; I see it in their faces. Be certain, however, that I intend to die without infamy, and the Cardinal will see that I care neither for him nor his tortures."

As soon as the prisoner had left the hall Laffemas produced a letter which he showed to the other judges. It came from the Cardinal, or rather from the King, and ran as follows :—

" If the Chevalier is condemned to the rack, let

this letter be shown to him; if he is condemned to death, suspend the execution."

De Jars was condemned to death, and was led out upon the scaffold, where he showed the most absolute calmness and courage. He defied his enemies and his judges, and prepared to meet his end with all firmness, trusting in God and committing himself to His all-gracious love and care. Having thus fortified his soul, he knelt down to receive the final blow, and then only was his reprieve produced. Dazed, almost without feeling or power of speech, and hardly knowing if he was dead or alive, he was led away, and Richelieu's vengeance was satisfied. The torture had not been meted out to him alone. The Queen, informed day by day of what was going on, lived in a state of extreme tension, and when the fatal day drew near could neither eat nor sleep. She swooned away when the news was brought to her of his reprieve, for she had already seen him in imagination a corpse on the scaffold, and she suffered almost as much as if the fatal deed had been actually perpetrated.

CHAPTER VI

THE POWER OF RICHELIEU

THE Queen and her friends thought that they worked in absolute secrecy, but they were shadowed wherever they went by Richelieu's agents, and at last Madame de Chevreuse determined to flee, thinking it preferable to remaining a prisoner.

On September 6, 1637, after a private and tender farewell of the Queen, she went out for her ordinary drive, taking care to go where most people should see her, so that her designs might not be suspected. She returned to the palace at dusk, and having changed her costume for that of a man, she slipped out of a side door, mounted her horse and rode off unattended save by two men, also mounted. The court beauty, who had been waited on from her childhood, found herself without her waiting-women, with no map of the country, not even a change of apparel, riding on the lonely and dangerous road in the starlight of that autumn night, hardly sure of the direction in which she was going. It was nearly dawn when they reached a château at Ruffec belonging to the Comte de la Rochefoucauld. She did not demand hospitality from him, though she knew well he would have carried out her slightest wish. Perhaps she feared to endanger his safety, but she wrote him the following note:—

"MONSIEUR,

"I am a French seigneur, and I implore your help. I have just fought a duel, and have been unfortunate enough to kill my adversary, a man of position. It is necessary, therefore, that I should leave France without loss of time, for they are already in pursuit of me. I know you are generous, and so I beg of you to lend me a carriage and a servant."

Whether the Count had any suspicion of the truth or not, like a true gentleman he at once sent the desired aid to the fugitive, and, worn out by her long ride, Madame de Chevreuse sank gratefully among the cushions of the coach.

In the middle of the second night she came to another house belonging to La Rochefoucauld. Here she left the carriage, and started for the frontier on horseback.

When she arrived there her saddle was covered with blood. She declared she had been wounded in the thigh, probably in an encounter with some of the marauding bands that infested the land, and weak from the loss of blood she dared go no further. She turned into a side path which led to an old grange, where she threw herself exhausted on a heap of straw. So lovely did she look as she lay, in the black velvet costume of a nobleman that she wore, that a good countrywoman who came by stopped full of admiration to look at the weary stranger.

"This is the handsomest boy I have ever seen," she exclaimed. "Sir, you fill me with pity; come, I beg of you, and rest at my house." It was difficult to get the good soul to understand that the youth she so admired preferred to be left in peace.[1]

In spite of all her hardships and difficulties, Madame de Chevreuse's courage and energy never deserted her. Her gay and buoyant nature rose above every trouble, and the thousand perils she went through only made her spirits rise the higher. She thought, too, of everything, and had already sent her jewels to La Rochefoucauld, partly that he might take care of them, and partly as a sort of legacy should anything happen to her[2] The mountain-passes and the gloomy defiles did not daunt her ardent mind—it is even said she swam one of the rivers—and she succeeded in reaching Spain, and was able at last to rest from her travels in safety. Once her arrival was made known, she received the greatest attention from the Spanish Government. As the intimate friend of their Infanta they loaded her with kindness. Her journey to Madrid was of triumphal progress, and Philippe showed her every attention in his

---

[1] Tallemant, *Extraits de l'Information*, vol. i. p. 250.

[2] *Extrait de l'Information faite par le Président Vigner de la sortie faite par Madame de Chevreuse, hors de France, Bibliograph National Collection Du Puy*, N°· 499.

power—indeed, report said, far more than was at all necessary for his sister's lady-in-waiting.

As to poor Anne, her little gleam of conjugal happiness was short-lived. To attempt to live in harmony with Louis was more than could be expected of her. She gradually grew accustomed to her life of solitude, and the practices of religion filled up her time, which was divided between pious acts and the gossip of her friends, who brought her the news of the day; she was not, however, surrounded by altogether desirable people. Sometimes she and they plotted against Richelieu, but these poor feeble women could do but little against that master mind. The saturnine Cardinal must often have laughed at their puny efforts—indeed, he held both King and Queen in the hollow of his hand. He treated the latter in the most arrogant manner. Once when the court was at St. Germain the Queen drove into Paris, and when she was near the Tuileries she met His Eminence's coach, he having just driven in from his country house at Rueil. He actually had the insolence to call out to the royal coachman to stop that he might find out what was Her Majesty's business. Anne naturally was furious, and ordered the coachman to proceed.

Richelieu was much offended at her taking such a tone with him; the Queen would not allow herself to be pacified, and, in the words of the faithful La Porte, " Il y eut un grand démêlé."[1]

But if the tyranny of Richelieu was galling to

[1] *Mémoires de la Porte*, p. 91.

many about the court, Louis was almost as great a sufferer from it as the rest. The King, under the thraldom of his favourite, had become a regular puppet. He led the most melancholy and miserable existence, without power, without a suite, without a pleasure. He lived mostly at Saint Germain like a private individual; and while his armies besieged towns and fought battles, he occupied himself chiefly in snaring birds.

He really was the most unhappy prince in Europe. He did not love his Queen, and felt nothing but aversion and coldness towards her, and at the same time he was a martyr to his passion for Madame de Hauteville, which possessed him entirely and added to his torments, for at times he suspected her of being in league with the Queen, and making fun of him and his attentions. He was jealous of the state and greatness of his Minister, though it was his own doing that the Cardinal had attained to such heights; and anger, first smouldering, then began to blaze up in his heart against the mighty Richelieu. All the same, he could not live without him, and was not happy a minute out of his sight. Jealousy was the keynote of his character, and never happy himself, he could not bear others to be happy either.

During the three years' war from 1635 to 1637, when the Imperialists penetrated into Picardy, and were within three days' march of the capital, there was a regular call to arms, and every man who could fight for the Sovereign enlisted at once. Among those anxious to do so was La Porte, and he begged the Queen to give him leave. Anne was in despair. He held all her secrets, carried all her letters, and she knew not how to do without him. While they were discussing the matter, the King entered the room, and, joining in the conversation, demanded of the Queen what were her objections. She dared not reveal her real ones, but pleaded need for his services. Louis, who was ever jealous of her faithful servants, exclaimed angrily, " I insist on it. La Porte shall go."

" It was but to annoy me," said Anne sadly when the King had left her [1]; but La Porte had to go. In his absence an intrigue in which he had been employed was discovered, and he was thrown into the Bastille, and the Queen, in extreme terror, made a full avowal of her fault to Richelieu, and signed a solemn engagement never again to commit a similar offence, whereupon the Minister promised in return to mediate for her a complete reconciliation with her husband. This was accordingly effected, and Richelieu once more triumphed. Every day his power increased. His rightful Sovereign had become his slave, and he held the proudest position in Europe, with the most illustrious monarch of the world at his feet.

[1] *Mémoires de la Porte*, p. 107.

CHAPTER VII

MAZARIN

A GRAND and brilliant reception was being held at the Louvre one evening. The long corridors were filled with all the flower of the French nobility. Wealth and beauty, jewels and court dresses rendered the scene a gay and sparkling one, and foremost among all was the Queen. The years as they had passed had added to her beauty, and she was considered one of the handsomest women of her day. She was then in her prime, with a fine figure, and that air of majesty which inspired respect and admiration. She had at the same time a very feminine gentleness, and a sweetness of disposition which lent a grace and charm to her attractions. Her beautiful eyes had already caused havoc among the hearts of men, and they had lost none of their power. As she moved among her courtiers in her royal robes and sparkling jewels, many an admiring glance was cast upon her.

Where she stood the centre of attraction, Cardinal Richelieu approached, leading towards her a stranger attired in the violet robe of a dignitary of the Church, and with that veiled insolence which the

Minister so often affected, he introduced him to the Queen, saying:

"Madame, you will like him; he has an air of Buckingham."[1]

Whether these words were said or not, this was the manner in which Guilio Mazarin and Anne of Austria were brought face to face, and from that day their lives were strangely intermingled. Of the early history of this man, destined to be so famous, the details are somewhat scanty. In 1601 a man of obscure family of the name of Pietro lived in a small village or bourg called Mazarino. His calling was uncertain; he has been diversely credited with being a manufacturer of rosaries, a straw-hat maker of Palermo, a fisherman, a banker, a Sicilian gentleman.

This very variety of titles shows how ignorant the generations to come often are of the social or business standing of unimportant personages who yet have left their mark in some shape or other on the world. Of one thing we may be certain—he was not a mere working artisan, and must have been possessed of a certain amount of worldly goods, for he aspired to the hand and married the daughter of his patron, Ortensia Ruffalini.

It is not known where the young couple settled down, nor where their firstborn saw the light. It was July 14, 1602, on which Guilio or Jules was born, some say in Rome, others at Piscina in the Abruzzi.[2]

[1] *Tallemant des Reaux*, vol. ii. p. 232.
[2] Amedée Renée inclines to the latter theory, and gives as his authority the *acte de batême*.

By this time the family, probably for their aggrandisement, had taken the name of Pietro's native village, by which they were henceforth known; but Guilio always signed himself Mazarini till he succeeded Richelieu as Minister.

He was educated at a Jesuit College in Rome, where he acquired the knowledge and train of thought which enabled him to enter the line of life which eventually led him to the highest dignities. In his youth he had no idea of joining the Church. He was a bright, clever boy, with a surprising memory, so that learning came easy to him; but at that time he was by no means a student or a candidate for religion. His passion was play, gaming being very prevalent in Europe at that time. Even in Rome under the eye of his father he indulged in this pastime, which probably was the reason why he was sent to Madrid, with the idea of studying law there.

But change of residence did not alter the character of young Mazarini. He entered into the amusements of the capital, and repaired once more to the gaming-tables, losing all the small fortune he possessed. He turned away from the card-table in despair, exclaiming, "A man without money is a senseless beast good for nothing!"[1] and it is hard to say what might not have happened to him at this crisis had he not been followed from the gaming-house by a Spanish notary, who from the interest that he took in

[1] Amedée Renée.

him must have known something of him or his family.

He offered him money for his immediate wants, and kindly pressed him to return to his own home with him.

"Though Mazarini could not know how momentous this step might have proved to him, it nearly changed the whole current of his life." In the Spanish home where he was so warmly welcomed was a charming senorita, the daughter of his host. Youth and beauty are drawn together as by a magnet. It took but a few days for the net to close in around him. The father offered to take him into his business, the girl's bright eyes flashed out a still more winning invitation.

Had the temptation caused Mazarini to consent, the whole course of history would have been changed. But the turbulent spirit within him craved for fresh excitement. The passion of gambling was still strong upon him; love may have attracted him, but domesticity did not. Once more he sought the tables, and this time won largely.

He was only a boy of twenty, so it was not strange that he allowed himself to be absorbed in the pleasures natural to his age; but to his credit be it said, he did not give up all else to this occupation. He might have become a mere devotee to cards, instead of which, having now the means, he gave himself up to study. His mind triumphed over his inclinations, his natural ability lifted him up, and having obtained the post of *cameriere* to a prelate, he was drawn once more into a clerical circle.

But a commonplace existence did not suit Guilio Mazarini; the hot blood within him surged up once more, and the adventurous life of a soldier next appealed to him. He joined the "Compagnie-Colonelle" of the Papal Army, and was given the rank of captain. He entered into his new career with zest, fighting being relieved at intervals by cards and dice, and only returned to Rome when the campaign was over.

Perhaps the tears and entreaties of his mother may have influenced him, for he laid down his sword and changed his soldier's habit for that of a civilian, and, the talent of which he had given proof so early having now the opportunity of developing, he joined the legates, and was sent on several diplomatic missions.[1]

Money now began to flow into his once empty coffers, and family affection, always a strong trait in his character, prompted him to help his sisters in every way possible. He made up a match between the eldest and Count Girolamo Martinozzi, and married the second, Hyeronyma by name, to Lozenzo Mancini. Their beauty had something to do with these excellent marriages, but more was owing to the name their brother by this time had made for himself. Indeed, the whole family had risen in the world, for Pietro's wife and

---

[1] When Richelieu came away from the first interview he had with Mazarin he said, "I have just been speaking to the greatest man the State has ever had" (Michaud, *Biblio. Universelle*).

the mother of his children being dead, he had married again, this time a lady of noble birth, Portia Orsini, of the House of Orsini.

Their success in life naturally brought down upon them the sneers of their less fortunate acquaintance, and Scarron, who passed as a wit, and was a poet with a biting tongue, wrote some satirical verses on the subject.[1] But those who rise can afford to overlook the jealousy of those they have left behind in the race, and take little heed of the ill-natured remarks their good fortune has called down upon them.

Mazarini must have always had a leaning towards the Church, at least towards its dignities, for he was favoured by Cardinal Barberini, who had taken an immense fancy to him, and had him appointed Nuncio Extraordinary to France. Mazarin, as he was now called, put on the violet robes and stockings of a Monsignore, which he never afterwards gave up, and he arrived in Paris with the state befitting his position, as well as his tastes, with a train of hangers-on and lackeys, and followed by a hundred and twenty-two carriages.

Many stories were told as to his first appearance in Paris society. One that has often been credited as true[2] was that he appeared at the Palais Royal one evening, and the lords and ladies who were gambling pressed the good-looking new

[1] " Fils et petit-fils d'un faquin,
　　Qui diffame la Casa Ursine
　　Par l'alliance Mazarine."
[2] *Mémoires de Retz.*

arrival to take part in the game. This Mazarin did willingly, in the hopes of attracting the attention of the Queen. His luck was so phenomenal that every one gathered round, watching the pile of gold growing beside him, and among the number was Anne. He continued playing till some 90,000 ecus had fallen to his share. As he rose from the table he pressed 50,000 ecus into the hands of the Queen's chamberlain, and begged him to present them with his profoundest respects to Her Majesty. She refused the gift at first, but the persuasions of the soft-voiced Italian made her at last give way.

This story is, however, most highly improbable, and has no good authority to support it. No man, whatever his position, would have dared to take such a step as this. The real moment, fraught with deepest importance, when Anne of Austria and the great Mazarin, destined to become lovers, first met, was when Richelieu, little thinking to what a high estate his new protégé would reach, presented him in the manner already mentioned.

At that time Mazarin was about thirty-seven years of age, ten months younger than the Queen. He had been well endowed by nature, as his many portraits prove.

He was tall and fresh-coloured, with a noble carriage. His features were large, his nose rather prominent, and his forehead lofty, token of the intellect of which he ever gave such proof. His hair was chestnut, colour his beard of a much darker hue, both with a natural wave. He is mostly depicted with a moustache. His eyes, deep and inscrutable, were always full of fire. He had beautifully shaped white hands, shaded by the lace frills of his sleeve, curiously like those of the Queen.[1]

As to his attributes, he was agreeable, with charming manners, a good raconteur, and a wit.

Such was the man brought in contact with this royal lady of Spanish birth. Of a passionate temperament, with little to occupy her idle moments and still less to fill the cravings of her heart, accustomed from childhood to live surrounded by gallantry and intrigue, it was a new life, full of momentous issues, which was thus opening before her.

Mémoires de Brienne.

CHAPTER VIII

THE CONSPIRACY OF CINQ MARS AND DEATH OF RICHELIEU

ON September 5, 1638, an event took place at St. Germain which fulfilled the hopes of the whole nation: the Queen gave birth to a son. If it caused the greatest joy to her people, it was a blessing sent from heaven for herself. She was menaced with much trouble, surrounded by many enemies, and had been humiliated even to the extent of having been made to sign with her royal hand a most humbly worded paper setting forth that she was guilty of all the charges brought against her; and with complete subjection she had been made to ask forgiveness of the King. This was not done without many tears, and very ungentle force was used to make her comply.[1] She was only supported by the knowledge that every one believed her innocent. Now her hour of triumph had come: she was a mother. France rang with joyous acclamations, and all hoped that the King her husband would now believe her word and take counsel with her.

But concord between them was impossible as long as the dark shadow divided them, in the person of

[1] Coll. Petitot, *Mémoires de Motteville*.

the hated Minister. Anne was too generous-minded to denounce him, too proud to seek his friendship. She could only trust to time relieving her from this danger, and her happiness was increased the following year by the birth of another son.

Louis had taken but scant notice of his firstborn; this second infant had a far larger share of his attention. He had never thought to be the father of two sons. Strangely enough, before he was three years old the little Dauphin was a source of annoyance to the King. Whether he disliked his heir, or whether he did not understand the ways of little children, nothing ever drew the father and son together. Once when the King had returned from a long day's hunting and was resting before the fire in the Queen's boudoir with a nightcap on his head, the little Prince, who was just learning to walk, toddled into the room, and not recognising his parent in that unfamiliar headgear, took him for a stranger, and burst into floods of tears. This annoyed the King most unreasonably; he made it quite a matter of importance, and complained about it to the Queen, declaring that the boy had drawn his fear and hatred of his father from the nourishment at her maternal bosom, a hatred which she had fostered in her children; should such a thing occur again both of them should be taken away from her.[1]

As to the "petit monsieur," as the second boy, Philippe Duc d'Anjou, was always called, he was a

[1] *Mémoires de Motteville.*

great pet with both his parents, and it would indeed have gone hardly with the mother had she been called upon to part with him. About this time an incident occurred which clouded with dishonour the last years of Louis XIII.

He had at that time as equerry the gay and brilliant Henri d'Effiat, Marquis de Cinq Mars, commonly known at court as M. Le Grand, on account of his appointment as "Grand Écuyer." He had been specially placed about the King's person by Cardinal Richelieu, and Louis had become extremely fond of him.

The King, when about to proceed with his suite to Nantes on some special business of State, took a fairly cordial farewell of the Queen, telling her to take care of the children, and never to leave them for a moment. There was little need for such an injunction. Anne stood smiling her farewells, with her little sons standing beside her, and wished the King a prosperous journey.

M. de Cinq Mars was of the party, and having like the rest a grievance against his former patron Richelieu, he took the opportunity of pouring his woes into the royal ear, and did his best to inflame the jealousy that Louis was known to display towards the Minister. Cinq Mars may have had good reason for his wrath against Richelieu; but the result of his endeavours to wreak his vengeance upon his enemy led to very serious consequences. The history of the conspiracy of Cinq Mars is too well known to all readers of Alfred de Vigny's famous romance to need repetition; he incited the King to rise in rebellion against his own State, under cover of the name of his brother, the Duc d'Orleans. The Duc de Bouillon was their chief adviser, but great projects were formed, founded on the notion that the Cardinal, who was very ill, would not live many days. False prudence brought about their ruin; Cinq Mars only half-trusted his royal master, and entered into an alliance with the King of Spain, on whom he thought he might rely for succour should Louis be too weak, and Richelieu prove too much for him.

At that time the Cardinal was lying ill at Tarascon, more or less out of favour, and hated by the whole country. But though weak in health, this crafty statesman was still able to bring his powerful mind to bear on the subject. Through M. de Chavigny he learned all about this treaty with Spain. Using him as a messenger, for his own weakness prevented him from moving himself, he was able to reach the royal presence, and M. de Chavigny persuaded the weak Louis, who was swayed first by one and then by another, that if Cinq Mars was allowed to proceed unchecked the throne would be endangered.

With a copy of the treaty before him, containing positive proof of his treason, the King could do nothing but order the arrest of Cinq Mars on June 12, 1642. Thus in a few hours the aspect of affairs was changed, and thanks to the skill of his envoy, Richelieu found himself once more in favour, and he lost no time in bringing his enemies to the dust. M. de Thou, his former personal friend, was to be made an example of, and the traitor Cinq Mars was doomed.

In his joy at having triumphed, Richelieu even made the King come from Narbonne to Tarascon to visit him at his bedside, and Louis, falling once more under his dominion, was willing to sacrifice without a murmur the man whom a few days before he had loaded with caresses. But if the story of Cinq Mars reflects little credit on the Monarch, it was a lasting infamy to the Minister. Almost dying himself, he took his prisoner in a boat attached to his own barge, and sailed up the Rhône to Lyons in the manner of the Roman consuls, who dragged their vanquished foes behind their chariot wheels. Cinq Mars and De Thou were brought to the scaffold together, and died with the courage so often displayed at such moments, in a manner worthy of their race. The King feebly intended to save Cinq Mars at the end, but was practically powerless to do so. The nation at large deplored his untimely death; ladies wept over his loss—none more so than Marie de Gonzague, who had loved him.

If Richelieu ruled over his Sovereign, he began himself to fall under the sway of another. Mazarin's star was in the ascendant. It was Richelieu who procured him the Cardinalate, and he had received his *barette* from the hands of Louis, February 25, of the same year.

In the Minister's growing weakness he felt the need of some one to lean on, and he daily turned to Mazarin for help and comfort. What memories must have assailed that death-bed! what tardy repentances must have agonised his soul! That vengeance over his enemies at Lyons was his last. His sufferings increased daily, and he was with difficulty brought back to Paris.

In the end he died like a saint, but he had not lived like a Christian, nor would he forgive his enemies, declaring to the last that he had none, that they were the enemies of the State.

He expired in the arms of the King, December 4, 1642, after having received the last rites of the Church, while Mazarin stood in solemn silence by the bedside and saw the only obstacle in the way of his own greatness vanish away.

It was said that Pope Urban VIII., when informed of Richelieu's death, exclaimed:

"If there is a God, he will be rightly punished; but if there is no God, truly Richelieu was a clever man."[1]

The late Minister left all his vast possessions to Louis, including his beautiful country place at Rueil.

That feeble-minded King was incapable of continuing without some support, and he turned at once to Mazarin for counsel. Regret for Richelieu he had none—indeed, he experienced the profoundest relief;

---

[1] "Ah! che se gli è un Dio, ben tosto la pagara; ma verame te se non c'e Dio, è glant uomo."—*MSS. des Mémoires de Motteville.*

but he was all the same ready to put his neck under another yoke.

The new Cardinal, as able a man as the last, saw his opportunity and took it. He did not terrorise Louis as his predecessor had done, but he made himself absolutely indispensable to him, and day by day his position was strengthened till it became impregnable. Richelieu's admiration of his talents had been so great that it was he who really placed him in power, declaring that Mazarin had more knowledge and zeal than any other person, and that he was the most capable man he had ever known.

Thus these two great Ministers, who ruled in succession, and who each remained in office for eighteen years, have gone down to posterity with their names linked together and their praises sung by at least one gifted poet.[1]

[1] " Tous deux sont revêtus de la pourpre romaine,
　　Tous deux sont entourés de gardes et de soldats,
　　Il les prends pour des Rois.
　　Richelieu, Mazarin, Ministres immortels."
　　　　　　　　　　　　　　Voltaire, *La Henriade*.

CHAPTER IX

DEATH OF LOUIS XIII. AND RISE OF MAZARIN

ACCORDING to La Rochefoucauld, it was during the short interval between the death of Richelieu and that of Louis XIII. that Mazarin began "to open avenues into the heart of the Queen."[1]

At first Anne conceived a great aversion to him, looking upon him as a creature of Richelieu; yet all the same his personal fascinations grew upon her; seeing that he sought to do her no evil, she by degrees gave him her full confidence. As he perceived that the King's health was rapidly failing, and that a long minority was in prospect, he knew it rested with himself to become the soul and centre of the Council, and he did not miss his opportunities.

Mazarin was still a young man, only forty years of age; he did not neglect his personal advantages, nor fail to put forth those refinements of manner which are paramount with most women. His cleverness then and afterwards consisted in seizing the unique moment. There was no plank more solid on which to launch himself than the heart of

[1] *Mémoires de la Rochefoucauld.*

the romantic and tender-hearted Queen; he put himself at Anne's feet as a means of reaching her heart.[1]

Therefore the Cardinal persuaded the King, or rather gently insinuated, that it would be wise to make the Queen Regent, because it would greatly limit the power of the Regency were it held by a woman.

When Louis realised that he was dying the court was at St. Germain. He felt that he had but a few hours to live, and, turning to M. de Chavigny, said, "Let us think of business," and then gave forth the reasons that had been already put into his mind. After Chavigny had written out the King's wishes, the Queen entered the sick room, and the dying Monarch made her read the paper and solemnly promise to observe his requests. He had intended to put into his declaration an order to the effect that the Chancellor Chateauneuf and Madame de Chevreuse should for ever be exiled from court, for, said he, rising with a last effort, and speaking in a clear voice, "Those two are the devil."[2]

But he lingered on for six weeks after that time, daily dying, but never able to depart. Many of those around him were wearying for the end, so little affection had he inspired, and so rife were the intrigues about him. To the last he was conscious, and died tranquilly May 14, 1643, in the forty-third year of his age.

Anne, kneeling by the bedside, burst into tears

---

[1] Opinion of Victor Cousin.
[2] MSS. of *Mémoires de Motteville*.

when they told her he had passed away, and she was gently led from the sickroom by her physician to her own apartment. She mourned him sincerely, and said afterwards that his death had caused her acute grief; her feelings towards him had ever been tender, and hers was not a nature to bear ill-will. Rousing herself from her natural sorrow, she repaired to the royal nurseries, where with streaming tears she saluted her Sovereign in the person of the tiny Dauphin, whom she clasped in her arms.

On the following morning Louis XIV. and his mother, accompanied by the Duc d'Orleans and the Prince de Condé, left St. Germain for Paris. The lying-in-state of the deceased King was held at the former place, and the Duc de Vendôme remained in charge at the Palace. The Duc d'Orleans and the Prince de Condé looked askance at each other for a time, and a rumour was current that Monsieur the late King's brother had intended to seize the person of Louis XIV., and thus quench for ever the authority of Anne; but she had taken her precautions against the evil machinations of the princes of the blood, and had doubled her guards. On their arrival in Paris, the roads were lined with thousands of people, and salutes were fired with all due honour. Anne was to be the saviour of her people and the happiness of France; in her arms was the young King, and her courage and gentleness through all her many persecutions had won the respect and love of all.

The new Minister, for such had Louis XIII.

promoted Mazarin to be, thought fit, however, to ask permission to retire to Italy. He was not yet sure of Anne. In his private letters of that date his want of confidence in her was very marked.[1] He therefore felt this was the wisest course open to him at the moment, and he demanded a private audience with the Queen.

Anne, possibly from personal reasons, certainly with the knowledge that the services of his Eminence would be invaluable to her, willingly granted his request, saying as she did so to the Comte de Brienne

"The Cardinal seems to consider himself offended; what can I do? He publishes abroad that he is asking permission to retire."

"Madame," replied the Comte, "if you offer him what he expects to have, he will be satisfied. If, on the other hand, he refuses you, it will be a proof that he will not live under any obligations towards you. In that case, you will lose nothing if he retires."[2]

Perhaps Anne thought the loss to her would mean a great deal, and she awaited with beating heart the entrance of the Cardinal.

As he bowed low before her, she tremblingly made her proposition, which was that he should remain as her adviser and Minister. The dark eyes shot forth their response as with his lips he thanked her for the great honour she was doing him, which

[1] Victor Cousin.
[2] Coll. Petitot, *Mémoires de Brienne*.

After Ph. Champigne.
ANNE OF AUSTRIA AS A WIDOW.

would, if possible, attach him still more deeply to her service; learning that she was acting on the advice of the Comte de Brienne, he expressed great pleasure.

After the funeral obsequies were over Anne, in her widow's robe, leading her son by the hand, appeared in state at the assembly, and declared that she appointed Cardinal Mazarin as chief member of the Council and Minister to the King.

Never did a regency begin more happily. The Duc d'Orleans could not, and therefore did not, contest her authority. The regencies under Catherine and Marie de' Medici had hitherto given satisfaction, but Anne of Austria was far more illustrious by birth than either of them; moreover, she had been appointed to her post by her late husband, and, holding as she did the affections of her people, she began her new reign without fear.[1]

Never had a court been so joyous, nor so full of anticipations of success and happiness. All those who had suffered under Richelieu's tyranny thought that they had but to ask to be rewarded for their sufferings, for, as they expressed it, "the Queen was so good."[2]

"On donnait tout, on ne refusait rien," said De Retz. Anne showered benefits, not always acting with the judgment which those in authority are bound to observe. She was yet ignorant of the price she

---

[1] M. A. Bazin, *France under Mazarin*.
[2] "The whole French language was comprised in five words, 'The Queen is so good.'"—*De Retz Mémoires*.

might have to pay for these liberalities, and when every one pressed round her, boldly asking for advancement, she had not the heart to refuse.

Anne was both inexperienced and incapable of serious work. She had spent a most idle existence, and, as she was naturally lazy, she found the cares of government a terrible burden. It was not long before she discovered that to rule over a country such as France was no child's play, and that alone and unaided it was practically impossible.

She had given all her confidence to the Bishop of Beauvais, her Grand Almoner, and had applied at Rome for a Cardinal's hat for him. He was a good man, but quite incapable of bearing the burden of State affairs. At first there was great friction between him and Mazarin, the Bishop having every intention to become Minister,[1] but he soon saw that the power of his colleague increased daily, and the Queen found it was necessary to withdraw her Almoner, much to his indignation, from her immediate circle. Mazarin remained humble and unobtrusive, drawing as little attention as possible to himself; under a quiet manner he hid his ambitions and his designs, and almost imperceptibly gathered together the reins of government. The cabal headed by the Duc d'Orleans and Messieurs de Vendôme looked with contempt, but no fear, at what they considered his presumption. But Anne, being a woman, understood him all the more easily from

[1] Michaud, *Biblio. Universelle.*

the first. Mazarin's mind was fertile in resource, and he was an indefatigable worker; he may not have had quite the genius of Richelieu, but he was the equal of his late master in diplomacy and administration.

He began from that time to come every evening to see the Queen, and hold a conference with her, though not in private. The doors were open where she sat to all comers, but the courtiers held aloof not to disturb the *tête-à-tête*, which began to be called "Le Petit Conseil."[1] Mazarin used to enlighten her about foreign affairs, of which she was ignorant, and of which he was a past-master, having studied foreign policy during his residence in Spain and Italy, as well as in France. He owed his Cardinalate to that knowledge, and had not studied under Richelieu to no purpose. It was not surprising that the Queen followed his counsels, and leaned upon his words. What other words were spoken at these evening meetings who can say? Lips and eyes both spoke probably, and the susceptible Queen was not long able to resist their influence. After the persecutions she had endured, and the indignities that had been heaped on her, it was natural that she should receive with delight the romantic homage paid to her, from the first hour of their meeting, by this fascinating foreigner. The writers of the day who clearly saw the situation admitted it from the first; if Anne had indulged in foolish

[1] *Mémoires de Motteville.*

flirtations hitherto, which had well-nigh wrecked her life, this time she was brought into contact with a man powerful enough to dominate her life, and strong enough to support her through all her difficulties.[1]

One reason that the Cardinal was accepted as Minister without open dissension was, that all knew that the late King had nominated him, and he sought to make himself popular from the beginning. He put back Chavigny into the Council as one of the Ministers, and told the Queen it had been an unwise move on her part when she turned him out. He also persuaded her that an act she contemplated doing, which would have ruined the relations of Richelieu, was a great injustice, and explained to her that as they would be, if left alone, dependent on her bounty, therefore they would serve her faithfully, and that for his part it was his duty to support all those who belonged to the man to whom he owed his greatness. His policy was so clever that he soon quenched all opposition from the Queen's adherents, and moreover he instilled into her heart the notion that these were acts of Christian virtue and clemency that would elevate her in the eyes of the world.

Notwithstanding her just aversion to Richelieu's memory, she rendered justice to his merits. One day when visiting his country palace at Rueil,

---

[1] "Mazarin avait sur Anne cet empire qu'un homme doit avoir sur une femme née avec assez de faiblesse pour être dominée, et avec assez de fermeté pour persister dans son choix."—Voltaire.

which he had left to the late King, she gazed at a fine portrait of him in the hall, and turning to the courtiers who surrounded her she observed · "Had this man continued to live his greatness would have gone on increasing."[1]

She upheld Mazarin on every occasion, and did not pay much heed to the advice of De Beauvais, showing by all her actions that she had given her entire confidence to the Cardinal.

France would have been spared many troubles, and the court would have been less full of intrigue, had those about her been able to share her belief in his virtues, and accept and admire his moderation and talents. But they preferred ambition to peace, and when they found the Queen had surrendered her authority to the Cardinal, a feeling of revolt towards him soon set in.

Among those recalled from exile by Anne was the Marquise de Senacé,[2] whom she desired to appoint as *gouvernante* to the King. As soon as it was known that this lady was once more in royal favour, crowds gathered daily at her house to pay their court to her. She received them in her bed, having been indisposed, and she afterwards said that she had been sitting up so long resting on her elbows occupied in bowing to all those who walked through her room to pay their respects, that the skin was absolutely excoriated!

---

[1] *Mémoires de Brienne.*
[2] Marie Catherine de la Rochefoucauld, widow in 1622 of Henri de Beaufremont, Marquis de Senacé.

The same court was paid to the Duchesse de Chevreuse, known to have suffered many things from the love she bore her Queen. She arrived from Brussels, where she had been well received, on account of the hatred that was felt in all foreign countries for her late enemy Richelieu. She had gone from Spain to Flanders, and she thought that the attachment which the King of Spain had felt for her would bring her more favour in the eyes of Anne; but she found the latter uninterested in the details of this flirtation, perhaps also secretly annoyed. Nothing lasts here below, and the fair Chevreuse found that the Queen was not quite the same as when they had parted. Anne no longer found the same charm in her former companion; she considered herself too devout and serious for her frivolous lady, and thought, moreover, that she was too much given to love affairs ill suited to her forty-five years.

The Duchess, on her side, found the Queen wrapped up in her babies; but more than all, she was Regent of France. The lonely, neglected young woman, Queen only in name, was now the most powerful lady in the land. Madame de Chevreuse shrugged her shoulders, and turned her attentions to another quarter. She had plenty of friends and admirers, and she had no fears that she would not succeed in some of her many intrigues. Her vivacity never flagged—indeed, it was her chief charm, for she was not, strictly speaking, beautiful, and absolutely lacking in wisdom; but her brightness and wit seemed to take the place of all other feminine attractions. She was the strangest mixture of want of judgment and brilliancy. It was De Retz who said of her, " Her devotion to love was her everlasting passion; she only changed the object of it." She amused and interested him, and he always called her " La Belle."[1]

Madame de Motteville, who upheld every action of the Queen, said that her devotion to her son the King filled her every thought; may it not rather have been that into Anne's heart was creeping an overwhelming passion, which left no room for friendship or any other sentiment? Besides, though the Cardinal tolerated the presence of Madame de Chevreuse, he had no mind to be supplanted by her, and took care to point out daily all her faults and little weaknesses to the Queen.

[1] " I found 'La Belle,' who had only just returned from Brussels, in tears at her toilette, as the Queen had ordered her to leave in twenty-four hours."—*De Retz Mémoires.*

CHAPTER X

MAZARIN AS MINISTER

ABOUT that time an adventure occurred which had the effect of placing the Cardinal more firmly than ever in his elevated position.

Women have often been the first causes in some of the greatest overthrows of States, and wars that threaten kingdoms and empires often do not produce such lasting effects as incidents brought about by the charms or malice of the daughters of Eve.

The Duchesse de Montbazon was considered the greatest beauty of the day. She was mother-in-law to the Duchesse de Chevreuse, and was, like her, in the cabal of the Vendômes, not so much on account of affection for her daughter-in-law, but because the Duc de Beaufort, a prominent member of it, was her lover. The two ladies were much of the same age, and great friends; Madame de Chevreuse, being furious because the Queen had ordered her away from court to her Château de Montrouge, was soon surrounded there by the enemies of Mazarin, and all those who had begun to complain of what they called the ingratitude of the Queen. Madame de Longueville, however, at that time belonged to the Queen's faction. She had been a

Princesse de Bourbon, one of the royal family, and had been forced by her father to marry M. de Longueville, who was enormously rich. But she never forgot the royal blood in her veins, and, though he was given rank directly after the princes, she would not consider him her equal. He was also very much older than herself; and as he was an admirer of Madame de Montbazon, there was no love lost between these ladies.

One day when the Duchess was entertaining guests in her own house, one of her ladies picked up a letter lying on the floor and carried it to her mistress; it was in a woman's handwriting, full of tender words to a beloved object. It was at once turned into ridicule, and made a subject of mirth in the little circle. From laughter to curiosity, from curiosity to suspicion, they soon passed on to conjecture, till at last they decided it had fallen from the pocket of De Coligny, brother of the Duc de Châtillon, who was known to entertain a passion for Madame de Longueville.

This princess had a great reputation for virtue, but none the less was by no means averse to admiration.[1] Of course the letter was in a feigned hand, and no one really believed in the statement made half in fun; all the same it reached the ears of Madame de Longueville, who resented the imputation greatly.

Though she had no special love for her husband,

---

[1] La Rochefoucauld gives testimony to her virtue, "Tous ceux qui essayèrent de plaire à la soeur de Condé, le tentèrent inutilement."—*Mémoires*, p. 393.

she was of course indignant at his attentions to the fair Duchess, and she also posed as being most correct in her conduct. She was also aware that the Duchesse de Montbazon had always intended to marry De Longueville when her old husband died, and had therefore been furious at his alliance with a royal princess.

Madame de Bourbon, mother of Madame de Longueville, now took up the quarrel, and went to the Queen to complain of the outrage. The whole court was in an uproar. The Queen took the part of the Princesse de Bourbon, and declared that it was her duty to see that the honour of Madame de Longueville should be vindicated; she gave her a personal interview, and promised her protection.

The Duc de Beaufort, who had always upheld Madame de Montbazon, now began to fail somewhat in his allegiance towards her. He had asked for the charge of the Admiralty, and when this was refused him he was extremely indignant, and laid the blame on Mazarin, for he declared the Queen had promised this appointment to him. But the Cardinal turned the enmity of the opposite party to his own advantage, for he had more wit than they, and knew how to make small incidents serve great ends.

He entered into the quarrel of the ladies, and when Anne ordered Madame de Montbazon to go and make a public apology to the Princess, it was Mazarin who wrote down for her what words she should say, and he appeared to be doing his best to satisfy both parties. The Queen and Madame de Longueville were in a state of extreme agitation, and made of this trifling affair a crime of *lèse-majesté*. The Duchesse de Chevreuse, being for many reasons on the side of her mother-in-law, helped the Cardinal to compose the harangue. They argued over every word. The Cardinal went from one to the other to adjust their differences, as if the peace of France depended on it. It was an absolute farce.

The following day the Duchesse de Montbazon was ordered to present herself at Madame de Longueville's to assure her there was no truth in the story of the letter, which had been invented by mischievous scandalmongers.[1]

Lest she should forget what she had to say, it was written on a piece of paper tied to her fan. She walked in with an extremely haughty air, and repeated her apology with a look that plainly said, " I attach no importance to what I am saying ! "

The Princess, however, had to accept it, only she begged the Queen so to arrange that she should never find herself in the same room as the Duchesse de Montbazon. This Anne promised.

A short time afterwards the Duchesse de Chevreuse gave a grand collation in a garden adjoining that of the Tuileries. It was called " Le jardin de Renard," as this portion of the garden had been granted to a man named Renard, who had

---

[1] The letter was really written by the beautiful Madame de Fouguerelles to the elegant Marquis de Maulevrier.—*Mémoires de la Rochefoucauld.*

been a lackey of the Bishop of Beauvais when he was Almoner to the Queen. This privilege had been a piece of royal favour, and it was one of the favourite places of amusement in Paris.[1]

On this occasion there had been some races, and the fête in question was held after the return of the gay world to Paris, and the Queen graciously promised to be present; she took Madame de Longueville with her, assuring her that she would not meet her enemy, as Madame de Montbazon was indisposed and keeping her bed. But as soon as they reached the garden, who should they see but the Duchess doing the honours in her capacity of mother-in-law.

"I implore you," cried the Princess, "to allow me to retire."

"No," answered the Queen, "I cannot allow you to do that, I will not subject you to this insult, but I know how to remedy the matter, though without destroying the harmony of the entertainment," and she at once sent word to Madame de Montbazon to feign sudden illness and retire.

This lady was so wanting in tact she actually refused to obey the command. The Queen, greatly offended at such conduct, firmly declined to take part in the collation after such want of respect being shown to her, and with the Princess returned to the Louvre in a state of great irritation. Next day the Duchess received the order to retire

[1] *Mémoires de Guy Joli.*

to one of her country houses, which she was perforce obliged to do.[1] Her disgrace was followed by that of the Duc de Beaufort, and the rest of their party, who had received the name of "*Les Importans*," on account of their arrogance, and the airs they gave themselves, which were intended as a contrast to the humility affected by the Cardinal.[2] Whether rightly or not, the Duke was accused of having laid a plot for the assassination of Mazarin in revenge for the slight offered to himself, but this may have been an exaggeration.

Those who adhered to the families now in disgrace declared that the Queen had made too much of a trifle; but the Cardinal was not sorry to profit by the Queen's anger to exile from court those interested in the cabal of the Vendômes. As to Madame de Chevreuse, disgusted at seeing her friends disgraced and ill-treated, she complained to Anne of the want of consideration she had displayed.

"I beg you not to interfere in matters that do not concern you," was the cold reply, "and leave me to govern my State and choose as Minister whom I please. If you will live pleasantly in France, and not mix yourself up in intrigues, you are welcome to stay, and on that condition alone will I extend my friendship to you."

---

[1] The order was sent in the King's name.—*Archives des affaires étrangères*, t. xv., p. 11.

[2] *Mémoires de Brienne*.

But the Duchess did not receive these remonstrances with the submission expected by Anne. She saw that the Queen's good graces towards her diminished daily, and it was no surprise to her when she, too, was requested to retire to her house at Tours. She had no intention, however, of being buried in the country, though she did not dare openly to disobey.

When she saw that Mazarin was quite as antagonistic to her as Richelieu had formerly been, she once more determined on flight, this time accompanied by her daughter. They disguised themselves as peasants, whether from necessity or from her love of excitement and adventure, and made their way to St. Malo. Here she threw herself on the mercy of the Marquis de Coetqueen, a nobleman of Brittany, who, as so many had already done, fell under the influence of her charms, and laid his fortune and his services at her feet. She had, however, the honesty to do by him as she had done by La Rochefoucauld, and left all her jewels in his hands, in case of her death, to repay him for his present assistance. A small vessel was secured, and they left that dangerous and rocky coast at the peril of their lives, hoping to reach England. But adverse winds drove them to Guernsey. The sufferings of the high-born nobles and ladies who crossed the stormy and uncertain channel, taking two or three days to do so, must have been great indeed. From there they eventually took ship to Flanders, and the

Duchess once more took up her abode among her friends in Brussels.[1]

The Cardinal must have looked upon these feminine quarrels—veritable tempests in a teacup—with amusement. But he managed to convey to every one with whom he came in contact that his own desire was to serve them and their interests. His insinuating manner enchanted men and women alike, save those who resented his authority and who felt the steel clasp under the velvet glove.

Even in his days of poverty at Rome he had been considered one of the most agreeable of men, so it need not cause surprise that he was able to please the Queen of France, and later on her two sons, by his deference, his charm of manner, and above all his tact. That he should have been hated as well is but the ordinary fate of a favourite.

But the foolish affair related above was not without serious consequences. A duel took place in the Place Royale between the Duc de Guise, one of the supporters of Madame de Montbazon, and the Comte de Coligny, in consequence of the letter attributed to Madame de Longueville. The victim of that Princess did not come off well in the combat, the Duc de Guise giving him a sword-thrust which caused his death shortly afterwards. It is said that Madame de Longueville watched the duel, hidden behind the window curtains of the

---

[1] *Extrait de l'information faite par le Président Vignier de la sortie de Madame de Chevreuse hors de France.—Biblio. Nationale, Coll. Du Puy*, No. 499.

old Duchesse de Rohan's house. If so, she must have suffered considerably, and her pride must have been deeply injured by the rhymes which were composed on the occasion, and sung and repeated in every direction.[1]

After this plot the Cardinal spoke very seriously to the Queen. In his own words he begged her " to throw off the mask and make a determined effort in her own defence, and trample these slanders under foot; while as to himself, he would fight with his back to the wall." [2] He reminded her of the insolence of Madame de Montbazon at the garden party, and told her it lay with herself to assert her authority.

At that time the Cardinal lived at the Louvre, the Queen having in full Council announced that owing to his bad health she wished to assign him an apartment in the palace, so as to converse more easily with him on matters of State.[3]

But now she made up her mind to leave the Louvre, having never really liked it as a place of residence, and took up her abode with her court at the Palais Cardinal, better known by its future name of Palais Royal. Here she fell ill of the

[1] " Essuyez vos beaux yeux,
Madame de Longueville,
Coligny se porte mieux
S'il a demandé la vie.
Ne le blâmez nullement,
Car c'est pour être votre amant
Qu'il veut vivre éternellement."
Mémoires de Motteville.

[2] *Carnets de Mazarin,* p. 96.

[3] *Lettre de Gaudin à Servien,* November 19, 1643, *Journal des Savants de* 1856.

jaundice; her physicians said it was owing to her sadness and sorrow.

The sorrows were mostly caused by the inability she felt to carry on the government, and to please every one. But as the malady subsided, she determined no longer to dwell on such things, but to put all her affairs upon the able shoulders of her Minister.

Armed with full power, he soon cleared away from the court people inimical to his orders. The Marquise de Senacé was the only person he had not appointed, and could not get rid of, on account of her position about the little King.

She was a tiresome woman, full of pretensions, and wishing to have everything her own way. She wanted to be made a duchess, and said that her children had the right to be princes, as they bore the name of Foix. However, like all unreasonable people, she was very unequal in her conduct—what the Spaniards called "altos y baxos"—so it did not trouble Anne much, and the Cardinal was equally indifferent to her acts of submission to his authority or her complaints at his orders.

CHAPTER XI

THE QUEEN'S LIFE AS REGENT

THE mourning being now over, the life at court resumed its usual course, and was carried on in accordance with the Queen's wishes. Anne was simple in her habits, but was very dainty in some of her tastes. It was impossible to find linen fine enough for her underclothing; she could not bear coming in contact with anything the least coarse. Once, when she was complaining of this, Mazarin said jokingly, " Madame, if you were ever to be eternally damned, your hell would consist in sleeping in coarse Dutch linen."[1]

An account of her daily life may be of interest, and is curious also as a picture of the great world at that time.

The Queen spent much time at her devotions. On holy days she was roused at nine o'clock, otherwise she always slept till ten or eleven. As soon as she was awake the principal officers and gentlemen came in to pay their court to her—a most unpleasing habit, and one which can hardly be understood in these days. They were followed by ladies, who came to discuss certain charitable institu-

---

[1] On her deathbed Anne lamented over the undue care she had bestowed on her bodily comfort.—*Mémoires de Motteville*, vol. 4.

tions in Paris, in which the Queen took much interest, for she was extremely liberal towards the poor and suffering. During these audiences, which were attended by men as well as women, she entered into many affairs, and conducted a good deal of business.

His Majesty the King, and *petit Monsieur*, were then brought in to play in her room, where they stayed till their midday meal was served, for they were not old enough to sit at table with her. After she had seen as many people as she desired, she would rise, and putting on a dressing-gown, retire to pray in her oratory; she then proceeded to breakfast with great appetite—the said appetite being rather astonishing. After a cup of bouillon and some cutlets, she was served with sausages and a sort of dish of boiled bread.

The little King was then allowed to hand her her chemise, which he kissed tenderly before presenting it, and this custom was continued by him for many years. When her women had put on her petticoats, she was wrapped in a long black mantle or robe called a *hongreline*, and in this costume repaired to the chapel to hear mass. She then returned to her room and completed her toilette. As has been mentioned before, she always did her hair herself, handling the beautiful chestnut locks with the greatest skill. Her white taper fingers, as they moved deftly over their work, were the admiration of those who looked on.

At that period of her early widowhood she wore no gold and silver embroideries, and but few jewels.

She also gave up rouge, which greatly enhanced the clearness of her skin. She could not have been very strong in health, for she often had to spend a day in bed to rest herself.

She rarely dined in state, but mostly alone with her ladies, and the little boys sat with her, though they were not allowed to partake of her dishes. After dinner she again retired to her oratory, and spent some time in prayer. In the afternoon she visited some of the charitable institutions already spoken of, and then returned to the palace to receive all the princesses and ladies of quality.

When this reception was over she retired to her own private room, where the Cardinal joined her, and he often stayed an hour or more. A large crowd of nobles and courtiers were waiting in what was called the *Grand Cabinet*,[1] and it was there that all the gallantries and intrigues arose between the ladies and gentlemen.

When that, to her, most precious hour of the day was over, she would walk, followed by the Cardinal, through their ranks, exchanging salutations and bidding them good-night.

Very few men had the privilege of the *entrée* to the Queen when in her private room. The Chevalier de Jars, Beringhen, the Marquis de Chandenier, Captain of the Queen's Guard, and his nephew and lieutenant, De Comminges, were of that number. Others tried often to make their way in, but Anne

---

[1] The exact meaning of the word "cabinet," so much used in old memoirs, is what would correspond with the modern word "library."

would scold if it happened often, and if she saw signs of their trying to take root there. The Maréchaux de Grammont, Créquy, and Mortemart were also privileged favourites.

As to the ladies, those generally in waiting were Mademoiselle de Beaumont, Madame de Bregy, and Madame de Motteville. The Duchesse de Chevreuse was absent, and Madame de Hauteville's place had also never been filled up, and though the Marquise de Senacé was a lady-in-waiting, her post was beside his Majesty.

When Anne had bidden the Cardinal good-night she again repaired to her oratory to pray. Supper was served at eleven, and then when she had finished the Queen retired, leaving her ladies to conclude their evening meal. An extraordinary feature of these otherwise luxurious times, we are told, is that the meal was not properly served for them. The ladies ate what was left, finished the Queen's bread, used her serviette, and drank up her wine, but the repast was otherwise a cheerful one, being free of all ceremony, and they laughed and talked freely among themselves.

The Queen had by this time finished her evening prayers, and her women trooped in, and sat for an hour or more amusing her with all the scandal they had collected during the day. The conversation was often very free as well as intimate and lively. Anne undressed in a leisurely manner, and often got into bed, where at last she became so sleepy—it being generally one in the morning—that she would dismiss the whole party, selecting one lady whose duty it was to sleep at the foot of her couch.[1]

Anne was extremely regular in her habits, and led this same life in Paris, Fontainebleau, and St. Germain. She held her Councils on Monday and Thursday, and was almost overwhelmed by the crowds who attended them. When in Paris she went to the mass at Notre Dame every Saturday. She received the Holy Sacrament every Sunday and feast-day, and fasted with great severity during Lent. On the eve of great festivals she always, when she could, went to sleep at Val-de-Grace, where she resolved to build a far finer convent, worthy of the Queen-Mother of Louis XIV. She would stay there two or three days at a time, retired from the world, living alone among the nuns, with only one bed-chamber woman in attendance. But though, as has been shown, Anne gave up a great deal of time to her devotions, she entered with much zest into more mundane occupations. She used to adore dancing, but that taste had departed as years grew upon her, and the dull life she had led for so long had quenched much of her former gaiety of disposition. But she still loved the theatre, though as long as she was in mourning she would only sit in the back of the box.

In fact, her life was a tedious one, and the Cardinal must often have found her a dull companion. She did not care for books, and had

[1] *Mémoires de Motteville.*

read very little; but her gentleness and goodness made up in a great measure for her want of wit and talent.

During the summer of 1644 Anne removed the court to Rueil to escape the great heat of the capital The nearness to Paris of this beautiful château, Richelieu's legacy to his King, made it very convenient. The gardens were lovely, and the children throve in the fresh air. In spite of its souvenirs Anne loved the place. She used to wander about in liberty free from the trammels of State, and took pleasure in the most innocent occupations. The Cardinal had sent to Italy for a certain Signora Lenore, a *virtuosa* whose voice was very fine.

The Queen would spend her evenings on the terrace in the starlight, listening to her singing. Doubtless Mazarin came often from Paris, and joined her there; the excuse being to hear his protégée sing, in reality to spend the summer evenings with the woman he loved.

But did he love her?

All through their history this question is forced upon us. As a woman, had Anne any attractions for him? At any rate he was in love with the Queen —in love with power and rank and influence, with the flattering of the crowd, and the cringing of the suitors. And it was Anne, and Anne alone, who brought him all these things. She was still handsome, still attractive, in spite of her forty-odd years, and above all she adored him.

Mazarin could not have been insensible to this, and so the summer days fled by in peaceful rest and dalliance; for these short weeks Anne was the woman, not the Queen, and tasted some of the joys of life.

Towards the autumn the court moved to Fontainebleau, which was always a favourite place of residence with Anne, who there sought such amusements as were compatible with her second year of mourning. But the pleasure of her stay was greatly spoilt by the news being brought to her one morning that the Cardinal was ill. He was staying in the palace at the time.

The Queen flew to his bedside in an agony of fear; all the affairs of State were at once laid aside. His malady was a fever, which was so violent that the courtiers felt sure he would never recover. Delighted at the idea of any change, they openly mentioned Chateauneuf as his successor. Some even had the audacity to speak on the subject to Anne The Comte de Brienne tried to soften it for her by saying that he did not think Mazarin was so ill as they tried to make out, but all the same she would do wisely in looking out for a safe man in case the Cardinal died.[1] But she could only wring her hands and wonder what would become of France and herself.

If the attachment between the Queen and the Cardinal had been only suspected before, there is no doubt that there were no longer any illusions on

[1] Coll. Petitot, *Mémoires de Brienne.*

Mazarin could not have been insensible to this, and so the summer days fled by in peaceful rest and defiance; for these short weeks Anne was the woman, not the Queen, and tasted some of the joys of life.

Towards the autumn the court moved to Fontainebleau, which was always a favourite place of residence with Anne, who there sought such amusements as were compatible with her second year of mourning. But the pleasure of her stay was greatly spoilt by the news being brought to her one morning that the Cardinal was ill. He was staying in the palace at the time.

The Queen flew to his bedside in an agony of fear; all the affairs of State were at once laid aside. His malady was a fever, which was so violent that the courtiers felt sure he would never recover. Delighted at the idea of any change, they openly mentioned Chateauneuf as his successor. Some even had the audacity to speak on the subject to Anne. The Comte de Brienne tried to soften it for her by saying that he did not think Mazarin was so ill as they tried to make out, but all the same she would do wisely in looking out for a safe man in case the Cardinal died.[1] But she could only wring her hands and wonder what would become of France and herself.

If the attachment between the Queen and the Cardinal had been only suspected before, there is no doubt that there were no longer any illusions on

[1] Coll. Petitot, *Mémoires de Brienne*.

Cardinal Mazarin
1654

the subject. Her grief and fear, and then her joy at his recovery, left little uncertainty in people's minds. Anne was over-anxious that every one should love her favourite equally with herself, and thereby she injured Mazarin's cause, for her efforts only resulted in his being hated.

The Cardinal understood French imperfectly, and many misunderstandings arose in consequence; he used to accuse persons of insolence, not being clear as to their meaning. Probably he affected this ignorance when anxious to separate the Queen from those he thought undesirable companions for her; he doubtless understood a great deal more than he admitted. He used to assume an air of authority and make very sarcastic remarks.

Once the Cardinal de Retz in the presence of the Queen told him that the animosity of the people against him was growing. Mazarin listened to these insinuations in silence, and then laughed scornfully. "I will tell you an Italian fable," he said: "the wolf swore an oath to a flock of sheep that he would protect them against his comrades, provided one among them would come every morning and lick a wound he had received. Your warnings are about as useful as the wolf's offers of protection, and I can take care of myself." He made light of his enemies, because in his pride he felt fully capable of holding his ground against them.

CHAPTER XII

THE QUEEN AS REGENT

IN the winter of 1644 the Queen of England, Henrietta Maria, returned as a fugitive to her own country. Such was the state of revolution in England that the poor Queen, on the eve of her confinement, could hardly find a place to lay her head. She, the most admired and richest of queens, had been reduced to such straits that she had to depend entirely on her midwife, Madame Peronne, for the veriest necessaries for the occasion. The King had taken her to Oxford, but, a siege being imminent, she had fled to Exeter, where her child was born; and only seventeen days after, she had once more to resume her travels, and eventually made her escape in a fishing-boat, and arrived more dead than alive in France. There she was received with the greatest joy by the people; for was she not a daughter of France, and aunt to their King? Anne was anxious to succour her with every mark of loving care, anxious to make up to her for the sorrows she had gone through, and, not being wanting in generosity, sent her own physicians to attend her, and loaded her with gifts.

Her kindness took a still more practical form, for she secured for her a pension of 30,000 livres a month. No one was more struck than Henrietta at the changes that had taken place since, as a young bride, she had left her country. Then, her own mother, Marie de' Medici, had been in full authority, and Anne, unloved and childless, and of no account, had been tyrannised over by her imperious mother-in-law. Now the Queen of England returned to find her brother and mother no more, while the despised Anne of Austria was Queen-Regent, with Mazarin at the helm.

Henrietta thought to enlist the Cardinal in her cause; but though he greeted her with the profoundest respect and sympathy, she soon saw that he had no idea of embroiling himself by meddling with the affairs of another kingdom.

During the winter the news came of the death of the Queen of Spain, the little "Madame" whose betrothal took place at the same time as Anne's. Her married life had been no happier than that of the Infanta of Spain; but like Anne, though unable to arouse any love in the heart of the King her husband, she was adored by his entire nation.

France was now disturbed by war. In 1645 the Duc d'Orleans and the Duc d'Enghien went with their combined forces into Bavaria. Hitherto the French troops had done nothing but hold their own, but they had gradually become inured to war, and were now to acquire fame under worthy commanders. The brilliant Condé had already, as Duc d'Enghien, given proof of his military genius—a genius for fighting battles—and with Turenne, the greatest strategist of the day, carried terror wherever he went. In the famous battle of Nordlingen, a great victory was won, but at the cost of an enormous number of lives.

A victory is the delight of a sovereign, and the Queen's eyes were sparkling with excitement when she heard of it.

"My brave generals," she kept murmuring. Those around her, filled with emotion at the news of the bloody encounter, knew not how to reply. At that moment the Cardinal appeared on the terrace where she was sitting, and all fell back before him. Anne rose, her face wreathed with smiles, and looked with dismay at his solemn countenance.

"Madame," he said gravely, "so many people have lost their lives, it does not befit your Majesty to rejoice at this victory." He raised his voice, desirous that those about them should be aware of his sentiments. The Queen looked abashed at this rebuke, and he proceeded to give her some of the harrowing details which she in her first excitement had overlooked. He read her the list of slain, and told her that the Duc de Grammont was taken prisoner, till at last the poor Queen was quite cast down.[1] A word of censure from Mazarin was always more than she could bear.

While these wars were occupying the attention of the princes of the blood, Anne and her Minister were occupied in the less congenial task of trying to raise money. The *Parlement* of Paris thought that during the Regency they might pretty well

[1] *Mémoires de Motteville.*

have their own way,[1] and when the Queen-Regent proposed to be present they replied she had no right to attend. This raised her ire, and she quoted the examples of the late Marie de' Medici, who when Regent always attended the opening in state.

As they could not come to any decision, it was determined to await the return of the Duc d'Orleans, and when the uncle of the King finally arrived a day was fixed, and everything was to take place with great ceremony. The Captain of the Guard visited all the prisons in the morning, as was the custom, and then appeared with the keys of the palace.

Anne rose early, and made an elaborate toilet. Her robes were still black, and her long black veil enhanced her stately beauty. She wore magnificent pear-shaped pearls, and huge diamond pendants, and a diamond cross of great value was suspended on her bosom. Many admiring glances were cast upon her. The roads were lined by companies of the guards and the Swiss troops, and they formed a wall on each side of the path that the King and the Queen were to take.

[1] In primitive times of the French monarchy the *Parlement* was simply the council of the Sovereign, in no way resembling our Parliament. In the time of Louis XIV. it was composed of 120 councillors, and comprised no less than seven chambers. The " Grande Chambre" was the highest court of judicature in the realm ; there were besides provincial *parlements*. As the Kings of France advanced towards despotism, the *Parlement* of Paris assumed more and more a political character. Under the stern rule of Richelieu, it was reduced to submissive silence ; but during the regency of Anne of Austria, the troubles broke out afresh. The President de Mesmes declared that " the *Parlement* held an authority superior even to that of the States-General, since by the right of *verification* they were judges of all that was there determined."

They walked together, she holding him by the hand; he was a pretty little boy with golden curls, and he smiled at those about him. Four of the Presidents came to meet their Majesties at the door of the Sainte Chapelle, and they went in to assist at the Mass. When they reached the great hall of justice they proceeded to the part appointed for them, and the King was lifted by his equerry on to the divan, called in the original "*Le lit de justice.*"[1] His mother placed herself at his right hand, and the Duc d'Orleans stood behind him. On one side were the dukes and peers and marshals of France, on the other were the principal ecclesiastics, headed by Mazarin. At the feet of the King the Duc de Joyeuse, his Grand Chamberlain, reclined. The Marquise de Senacé stood on the left hand of the King, nearest to him of all, doubtless to keep him in order, and to ensure his doing what was necessary.

When all were in their places the little King bowed, and looking at his mother, to make sure of her approval, said in a clear voice:

"Gentlemen, I have come here to speak to you of my affairs. My Chancellor will make known to you my royal will."

His clear childish treble, ringing through the

---

[1] The "*lit de justice*" was the ceremony by which the Kings o France compelled the registration of their edicts by the *Parlement*. *In curiâ Regis* might stand for it, but the thing never existed in England. It best corresponds to a pontifical pronouncement *ex cathedra*. The actual *lit de justice* was a royal seat or divan under a dais.

hall, filled his audience with delight, and the acclamation that followed was loud and long.

When the noise had subsided, the Chancellor, in an eloquent speech, represented the necessities of the State, pointed out the glorious victories of their army, and the desire of the Queen for peace. M. Molé, the First President, replied, praising in high terms the Regent, the wisdom of the Ministers, and the valour of the princes of the blood.

As soon as each principal member had held forth to his own satisfaction, and each in praise of the other, the King and Queen departed, in the same state with which they had arrived.

Anne, on her return, went straight to bed. It must have been the lack of comfortable sofas, and the habit of receiving company in the bedroom, that caused the ladies of that day to seek their couches on every possible occasion. As soon as she was comfortably settled, and had dined, the Cardinal arrived and spent the evening with her. All her women remained within call, but at a distance so as not to disturb them.[1]

Anne asked him if he had not been pleased with the little King, and they then discussed affairs of State together. Later in the evening others joined them, and sat in a circle round the royal bed. The conversation then degenerated into gossip, and they talked of the marriage of Mademoiselle de Rohan, and other matters of court interest.

[1] *Mémoires de Motteville.*

CHAPTER XIII

MARRIAGE OF PRINCESSE MARIE

THE autumn of the year was spent as usual at Fontainebleau, where the chief topic which occupied the attention of the court was a marriage which excited a great deal of talk.

Ladislas Sigismund, King of Poland, had aspired to the hand of Mademoiselle d'Orleans. This young lady received his advances with the greatest contempt, and laughed at the idea of marrying such an old suitor—troubled, moreover, with the gout, and living in a barbarous country. The old Monarch, bent on finding a wife, next turned his attentions to Mademoiselle de Guise, but the Queen raised objections to this. Undaunted by his ill-success, the King now sought out the Princesse Marie de Gonzague. She was the second daughter of the Duc de Mantoise, her elder sister Anne was well known as the Princesse Palatine.[1] She had been long about the French court, and was past her first youth, being thirty-three years of age, but she was still extremely handsome.

Monsieur, brother of the late King, when he was heir to the throne, had been desperately in love

[1] Coll. Petitot, *Mémoires de Brienne*.

with her, but his mother, Marie de' Medici, had interfered, having other designs for him.

Naturally this fine match coming to nothing caused a great deal of annoyance to Marie. There was some talk then of her marrying the King of Poland, but he chose a German princess instead.

Foiled in this second matrimonial attempt, she remained in Paris, giving herself up to a life of gaiety and amusement; but in the end she lost her heart, and gave all her love to the fascinating Marquis de Cinq Mars, and his tragic end plunged her into despair. This episode also had the effect of casting some discredit on her; it humbled the pride of her noble house.

Her friends saw in this possible marriage with the King of Poland, who was now a widower, a chance of reinstating her; and the Queen and the Cardinal were applied to, to aid in the matter. Mazarin, thinking that this princess, who had had nothing but misfortunes, would be eternally grateful to him if he raised her to the rank of a sovereign, made every effort on her behalf.

The Polish ambassadors were received at Fontainebleau by the Queen with due ceremony. The embassy was unlike any that had been received at the court of France. They appear to have been semi-savages; the envoys wore no linen, nor did they sleep in sheets, but went to bed naked, wrapped in furs. Their heads were shaved, and they were very dirty.[1]

Princesse Marie, who was among the ladies

---
[1] Bazin de Raucon, *Histoire de France sous le Ministère de Mazarin.*

seated in the room, rose hastily when they entered, and slipped away into the background. She wished to hear, but not to be seen; but some one of the party who knew her by sight pointed her out to the ambassadors, and they all turned towards her, and made her the most profound salutations. Laughingly, Marie felt constrained to come forward, and the somewhat disgraced lady-in-waiting found herself suddenly treated like a queen.

The next day a grand supper was given in the King's name to the envoys, and the contract was signed in the royal apartment, though her position was unchanged in the household, in spite of her coming honours.

Owing to a relaxation of etiquette at Fontainebleau, or perhaps to the number of servants being insufficient for state ceremonies, a curious incident arose, such as would hardly be expected in the palace of Louis XIV. Owing to a dispute among the retainers, there was no bouillon for the first course;[1] moreover, the lighting of the great staircase was overlooked, and the ambassadors had to grope their way to the King's chamber. It had been forgotten that they would certainly come that way, although it was not used ordinarily. Anne, after having scolded those in fault, began to laugh, and said that France was never ruled properly in great things or in small, and every one must have patience.

King Ladislas sent the Palatin de Posmanie

[1] *Mémoires de Motteville*, vol. i.

and the Bishop of Warmie to marry the Princess by proxy, and escort her to her new kingdom.

On the eventful morning the beautiful Marie, in a bridal robe, came into the Queen's room to show herself. She wore the pearls and diamonds which were the gift of Anne, and held in her hand a crown of priceless jewels. Behind her was carried the royal mantle of Poland—white velvet, embroidered with great gold flames.

"Look, your Majesty," she exclaimed, "they tell me I should wear these. What am I to do? My dress was not made for a mantle, it is too short; and should I put on the crown?"

Anne was amused at the new Queen's dilemma.

"You cannot wear the crown yet, dear child, it is not yours," she answered, "nor is the mantle necessary, for this is not a State ceremony."

The Cardinal, who was standing by, looked on smiling, as Marie held up the crown for him to see, and said she owed it to him. She then thanked the Queen very prettily for all her many kindnesses.

Anne was still attired in her black robe and veil, with ropes of pearls round her neck. She led the bride, in her simple white-and-silver dress, to the private chapel at the end of the long gallery. The only persons present were the King and "petit Monsieur," looking on with childish curiosity, and also the Duc d'Orleans.

His presence doubtless aided Marie to feel that, after the insult he had put upon her, her triumph had now come in spite of him : she was destined to wear the closed crown of royalty—and was really standing on the steps above him who had scorned an alliance with her.

It was the bishop who placed the diamond crown on her head at the end of the ceremony, assisted by Madame de Senacé, who was in attendance on the children, aided by the royal hair-dresser : it was verily, as Anne remarked, not a State ceremony.

The two Queens then dined together, her Majesty of Poland placed at the right hand of the little King. He was allowed to dine with his mother on this occasion, but " petit Monsieur " was too young, and was carried away to his nurseries. The bride then received such persons as desired to be presented to her. The Abbé de la Rivière, meaning to pay her a compliment, but with very bad taste, said it would have been far better if she remained in France as Madame.

Marie proudly raised her head, and in a clear voice, that all might hear, replied :

" It was destined that Monsieur should remain in France as Duc d'Orleans. My fate was to be a queen, and I am happy and content."

Anne, who loved any excuse for a dance, gave a grand ball in honour of the occasion. The great hall of the Palais Royal, considered the finest ballroom in France, was the scene of revelry.

Every delicacy was served at the supper, among others large baskets of sweet oranges and citrons, fruits which probably the envoys had never been acquainted with in Poland, and they were invited to carry them away.

The new Queen wore black velvet embroidered with gold, but the general opinion was that the dress was too heavy. The King, who could already dance very nicely, led her out.

She shortly after prepared for her departure, and took a courteous farewell of all her friends and foes alike. She kissed all the ladies of quality, and begged them to be seated in her presence. Indeed, she clung to her old friends, in spite of her new regal airs, for, with the future all unknown, she dreaded leaving for a strange land.

She was accompanied by the Duc d'Elbœuf and the Maréchale de Guébriant, also with a suitable following.

At first her progress was one of triumph, all along the road after passing the frontier of Poland, but the pleasure was somewhat lessened when at last she found herself in the presence of the King. He was old and gouty, and enormously fat; being unable to move about with comfort, he received her in Warsaw without any ceremony. He awaited her in the cathedral, seated in a chair, from which he did not attempt to rise. She knelt before him and kissed his hand, but he showed no pleasure whatever in seeing her, he looked at her fixedly, and, turning to the Ambassador de Bregi, who was standing beside him, said aloud:

"Is this the beauty of whom you gave me such a glowing description?"

Marie stood aghast at this reception. Weary and travel-stained as she was, she thought there might possibly be some reason for the King's remark, but none the less she was cruelly mortified. Old Ladislas then left his chair and walked to the altar, where the happy couple were promptly united, he then sat down again for the rest of the service.

Their Majesties repaired to the palace and supped together, but the food struck the Queen and the Maréchale de Guébriant as abominable, both in appearance and taste.

As the evening wore on she was terrified at all she saw, and whispered to her lady that it would be better if they returned to France. The King never uttered a word to her, and went off to his own rooms.

Madame de Guébriant lost no time in giving vent to her feelings, and assured those in authority that France would greatly resent the manner in which the new Queen had been treated. She declined to leave till she had seen the King show some mark of liking and respect for his wife. Seeing that evil consequences might arise, he agreed to do so, and took her to live with him as his wife, and paid her some attention in public.

Queen Marie parted with Madame de Guébriant with many tears, but tried to console herself with the grandeur and wealth that was now hers. In Poland it was the habit for the subjects to give magnificent presents to the bride of their Sovereign, and she was laden with rich gifts.

With this cold comfort the unfortunate lady had to make the best of the life before her, and it was far from a happy one, but she earned the goodwill of her people, as well as of the rest of Europe, by the noble use she made of her riches, and the courage and firmness she ever displayed.

CHAPTER XIV

GROWING ATTACHMENT OF THE QUEEN AND CARDINAL

THE life at the court of France continued for some time without any great change occurring in the lives of those intimately brought together. Anne, happy in the society of her Minister, and leaning on him for advice and support, passed her time pleasantly according to her own taste.

Her natural amiability caused her to be agreeable to those about her, and she, at least, did not perceive the smouldering hatred displayed towards the too powerful Cardinal. But the absolute power she put into his hands lessened her own, and in her desire that he should be beloved she failed to see that by her perpetual praise of him she defeated her own ends.

Mazarin had acquired an ascendancy over the Queen, and, whether he truly loved her or not, knew well how to give her pleasure. He sent to Italy for musicians and comedians, as the theatre was the thing she preferred above all else in way of relaxation.

These comedies were entirely musical pieces, and were, no doubt, the beginning of the Opera, which was not fully known or appreciated till the following century. Besides the Italian pieces, French plays were much in vogue.

The court used to assemble most evenings in the small theatre of the Palais Royal, where the Queen had a private box which communicated with her own room. She used to bring the King with her, and the Cardinal, and any persons to whom she wished to pay special politeness.

This love that the Queen displayed for the Play so upset the good Curé of Saint-Germain that he came himself one morning to see Anne, and told her that in countenancing the stage she was committing a mortal sin, and he brought her a document, signed by six ecclesiastics of the Sorbonne, to the same effect.

Evidently the presence of the Cardinal in the royal box in no way condoned the evil in their eyes.

This upset Anne very much indeed, and she applied to the Abbé de Beaumont, tutor to the King, for spiritual advice and assistance. With the aid of ten other learned priests he was able to prove to her satisfaction that, if nothing was said in the play contrary to public morals, there was no harm in the pastime, and that the rules of the Church were no longer so strict as had been necessary among the early Christians.

In this manner the Queen's conscience was set at rest. The courtiers laughed at the Curé and turned him into ridicule, and, moreover, declared the whole thing had been got up to throw discredit on the Minister. This last assertion was very likely true, for a conspiracy, political and religious, had been formed against him in the convents, said to be in the interests of heaven and the care of religion. The Cardinal was supposed to tolerate Calvinism, among other things. The idea that the Queen at the age of forty-two was in love with an Italian and a cardinal of Richelieu's making, was more than the sanctity of the communities could endure. Mazarin himself writes at this period, "All the convents are against me, particularly that of Val-de-Grace."[1]

Anne, ever since her children were born, had spoken of her great desire to see them well educated, and as she was of opinion that the Cardinal possessed the profoundest intellect in Europe, she determined to place the education of the King in his hands. She left the choice of the tutors to him, and the Marquis de Villeroy was selected, with the Abbé de Beaumont under him.

The poor little boy seems to have been put through a rather severe course, considering his tender years, for we read of him translating the Commentaries of Cæsar. He also learnt to draw and ride and dance, besides being proficient in drill.

In November the Queen received the news of the death of her nephew, Don Balthasar, only son of her brother, Philip IV. of Spain. For his sake she expressed great regret, but all the same she discussed the question of her own right to the throne of Spain in the event of her brother's

[1] *Carnets de Mazarin*, 11e, p. 62.

death, and she would hardly have regretted to see her second son succeed to that kingdom. For herself she cared little, but she was ever ambitious for her children.

The Cardinal now turned his attention for a while from grave matters of State to lighter ones, and at the end of the Carnival of 1647 he gave a splendid entertainment, which was received with boundless applause.

Of course the principal feature was a comedy to suit the Queen's taste, and the piece, which was called *Orphée*, cost 400,000 livres to put on.[1] He sent to Italy for a troupe of well-known singers, and special machinery and scene-shifters. Unfortunately all these preparations took so long that it was nearly the end of the Carnival before it was ready; as the idea was to give many performances, the Cardinal and the Duc d'Orléans pressed the Queen to sanction it being played through Lent in her presence.

But where her conscience was concerned Anne was always firm, and she refused. It was pain and grief to her to do so, especially as Mazarin displayed a great deal of ill-humour on this occasion. His open displeasure caused much satisfaction among a certain set, who hoped that it might tend to lessen his influence over the Queen; but though Anne held firm, and braved his anger, nothing that Mazarin could do made any real difference to her. Ever self-sacrificing, she solved

[1] Bazin, *Histoire de France sous Mazarin.*

the difficulty by retiring when the piece was half over, so as to have time for her prayers and go to bed early, so that nothing might interfere with her attending Mass the following morning; and it was only the first performance that she saw from beginning to end.

The following day the Cardinal gave a ball in the theatre, by means of a movable floor, which could be adjusted in a few moments. Panels with beautiful views and gilded frames were fixed all round, so that all semblance of a theatre had disappeared. Seats as if by magic lined the walls, and a throne rose up at the end of this wondrous hall—that is to say, a platform, with chairs under a canopy of cloth-of-gold. Great crystal chandeliers illumined the brilliant scene.

The Prince of Wales,[1] having joined his mother Henrietta Maria, was present, and was treated with much attention. The little King refused his own seat so as to place himself on an equality with his exiled cousin; Mademoiselle d'Orleans was made the queen of the fête, and seated in what should have been his own place.

She was covered with jewels, the Queen having adorned her with her own hands, and in her hair were diamonds tied together with red, white, and black ribbons. The King also wore crimson feathers and ribbons on his black satin habit. He was now eight years old, very well mannered, and danced to perfection.

[1] Afterwards Charles II.

The Duchesse de Montbazon had a crimson plume resting on her hair, it being the colour of the evening; her mature beauty showed to great advantage. The maids of honour, Mesdemoiselles de Pons, Querchy, and Saint-Martin, were thoroughly enjoying their flirtations and conquests, and hoping to find among some of the gallants who fluttered round them husbands suitable to their desires and ambitions.[1] Tongues now began to wag freely, and many scandalous stories were current over the relations between the Queen and Cardinal. The episode between Anne and Buckingham, which had been grossly exaggerated at the time, had never been forgotten. Her calumniators strove to make out that she was a light woman, ready to welcome one lover after another. Her historians may exonerate her from that charge, but her passion for Mazarin is admitted by all.

To give a pretext for their long and intimate conversations, the Cardinal introduced a change in the household, and elected to be almoner for her private charities.[2]

It was the Duc de Beaufort who first had his eyes opened to the growing intimacy between the Minister and the Sovereign, and told it in confidence to the youngest son of the Duc de Vendôme. Mazarin had long tried to win over these princes; it was with him a regular system to begin

---

[1] *Mémoires de Motteville.*
[2] *Carnets de Mazarin*, p. 96.

in the first instance with his powers of seduction, and when all the amiable means were exhausted to proceed to more vigorous measures. But neither method was successful, and the Duc de Vendôme turned a deaf ear to the Cardinal's blandishments. Anne was aware of the feeling against her. One day she found a note on her table, containing these words, "Madame, if you do not get rid of the Cardinal, others will get rid of him for you."[1]

She taxed La Porte, the valet, with having placed it there, but the man denied all knowledge of it. He was a faithful servant and depository of all the Queen's secrets, but at the same time he considered it his duty to remonstrate with her.

One afternoon when Anne happened to be alone, she was looking listlessly out of the windows—it was a wet day—with an air of great *ennui*. All at once she beckoned to her valet, who was watching his mistress with affectionate solicitude, to come forward.

"What do they say of me, La Porte?" she asked abruptly.

La Porte looked rather sheepish. He found it a difficult question to answer, but the Queen was insistent.

"If your Majesty insists on knowing," he stammered, "all the world is talking of you and his Eminence. In fact, people talk of little else."

Anne flushed scarlet, and turning away, began to drum angrily on the window with her fan. The

[1] *Journal d'Olivier d'Onnesson*, vol. I, p. 101.

servant stood in an attitude of humble respect, while his lady with difficulty restrained her anger; the quick movement of her fan was only evidence of the wrath within.

What! Was she obliged to defend her conduct, in the eyes of men, as if she were a common grisette? The flaming colour in her cheeks told its own tale as to her resentment, yet she could not vindicate herself; and she stood convicted in the eyes of her own menial.[1]

When once the matter began to be voiced and put into a solid form, instead of a mere hint, it was a source of great anxiety to both the Queen's friends and enemies.

Madame de Brienne, mother of the Count, an old lady who loved Anne well, was deputed to remonstrate with her.[2]

Full of motherly tenderness, she first asked the Queen to allow her to join with her in prayer, then, feeling that frankness was the only possible means by which she could approach the subject, she openly told her Majesty what rumours about her were spread abroad.

Anne listened in silence with burning cheeks. Determined to emulate her old friend in frankness, she replied in a calm voice: " I own that I am fond of Mazarin, and I admit that I have not been sufficiently prudent—though it is a calm and tender affection, devoid of all passion; but now, here

---

[1] *Mémoires de la Porte.*
[2] *Mémoires de Brienne.*

in my private oratory before the altar, I renounce this friendship that was so dear, and our relations will never go beyond what is necessary for the affairs of State."

"Will you swear to this, Madame?" cried Madame de Brienne, in a voice trembling with emotion.

"I swear it," replied the Queen.

But, alas! the oaths of lovers, as of gamesters, are written in water, and are but rarely kept.

Poor weak Anne meant to do right, but she was as a bird in a fowler's net. She determined to have a thorough explanation with Mazarin, telling him all that had been said, and frankly discuss the situation with him.

It does not need a very profound knowledge of the human heart to be certain that, after listening to the Cardinal's tender warnings and specious reasonings, the Queen had sunk yet deeper into the abyss on the edge of which she had been standing, and Mazarin left the royal presence with the knowledge that the Queen was more firmly his than ever.

As to his own feelings, it is impossible to gauge the depths of his affections; for though love was true on her part, it must have been more or less simulated on his. If later on, as his contemporaries hint, he passed beyond and triumphed over the scruples of the Queen, it was because he saw in that the surest means of government. Ambition, not love, ruled Mazarin's conduct.

The year drew to a close with deep anxiety at

court. One evening in November the King, who was playing at cards, apparently in the best of health, suddenly threw them down, and told his mother that he felt ill. It was not thought to be of much consequence, but by the next day he was in a high fever. The Queen was in despair, and sent off at once for Monsieur, his Majesty's uncle.

After two days, the doctors pronounced the malady to be small-pox, that scourge which ravaged alike the Palace and the hovel, and from which neither kings nor peasants were exempt. All the beauties of the court, at least those who had so far escaped having the malady, fled from the Palace. "Petit Monsieur," who had been ill for some time, and was in rather a weak state, was promptly sent away. It was always supposed that Anne loved her little son the best of the two, but she displayed far more feeling on this occasion than she had done when he was ill. She never left the King's side, and though the disease ran its course without any complications, she fell ill herself from extreme anxiety.

The Cardinal meanwhile was watching the case with deep concern, though of a different nature. What would happen should young Louis die, and the Queen-Regent become seriously ill? It was thanks to himself that she had greatly lost her hold on the affections of her people; and as in the event of the King's death it would be necessary for her to be re-elected Regent, the Duc d'Orleans might take advantage of such a crisis to elevate himself to power.

The subtle Italian was, however, always prepared for emergencies, he worked quietly to gain those about the person of the duke, so that, by promises of advancement, he might bind them to his services.

But his precautions were not needed; by Christmas the King was pronounced to be well, and his little brother was brought back. When the child saw his former playmate he did not recognise him, for Louis' face was still red and swollen. But so prevalent was the disease, and so many people were marred by it, that it was not considered such a blemish as at the present time. Deep pock-marks after the inflammation had subsided were a very ordinary spectacle, and not much attention was paid to the disfigurement.

CHAPTER XV

MAZARIN'S PALACE

WHILE the court was still in residence at the Louvre, the Cardinal, by way of giving himself more independence, purchased the Hôtel Tubœuf, which was situated at the bottom of the garden of the Palais Royal.

At first he had been satisfied to live in the Hôtel St. Pol, then he accepted an apartment in the Louvre, but now he required something more.

Two centuries ago this quarter of Paris was not, as now, a mass of bricks and mortar, with houses six stories high, and rows of shops beneath. Then it was a most lovely and charming suburb, with extended views over the surrounding country. He had long had his eye on the Hôtel Tubœuf, and when the Queen moved to the Palais Royal he was able from her windows to judge of the effect of the coveted estate.

The president Tubœuf was only too pleased to get into the good graces of the Minister by selling him his house; it was even said that Mazarin won the hotel from Tubœuf at picquet; but this was a fable, for he mentions several times in his notes how he acquired the house, and how much he had paid on account.[1]

[1] Among his papers were found in his own writing these words, "La meta per la mia casa a M. Toubœuf."—*Biblio. Roy. Fonds Balrize,* p. 77.

But once he had taken possession he did not find the building at all up to his requirements, and he consulted his architect, François Mansat, to make some improvements. He ordered a grand double staircase to be built, with a courtyard with double ingress and egress, and also planned a wing on the ground floor opening on the garden, the rooms of which were for his collection.[1] Accustomed to frescoes in Italy, he did not like the cold nudity of French buildings; he required more colour. He also drew a sketch or plan of his requirement; this was known to have existed, though it cannot now be found.

He wanted all the beauty of Rome in Paris, but nowhere in that city could he find the necessary artists—none were clever enough to please him. Therefore he sent for Romanelli and Grimaldi, who had decorated the Vatican.

It is two hundred and sixty years since those two Italian painters fixed the memories of their sunny land on the walls of the Palais Mazarin. One adorned it with landscapes, the other with mythological groups.

The gallery was painted from the roof to the parquet, and filled with the choicest articles. Tables of lapis-lazuli, mother-of-pearl, and gold, ebony and tortoise-shell cabinets, alabaster and porphyry figures and a wonderful ivory bed were among the art treasures.

Though Mazarin had sent so far for his

[1] La Borde, *Palais Mazarin*.

From an engraving by Nanteuil after Chauveau.

CARDINAL MAZARIN IN HIS GALLERY.

decorators, it was not that he wished to slight the land of his adoption. Later on he favoured French artists, but at the first he did not consider them up to his standard, for it was one of Mazarin's merits that he encôuraged art and protected painters. This beautiful private palace was soon the talk of Europe, and the eyes of the world were drawn towards it. He now turned his attention to another department. His stables were said to be the finest in Europe, they extended the whole length of what was afterwards the Rue de Richelieu. There were three great entrances to the building, and seven inner courts, while the façade was richly adorned with sculptures and Ionic columns. He sent to Italy for his carriages, the art of coach-building having attained to great perfection there. He loved his horses, which mostly came from England, and had also Spanish mules which sometimes drew his coach, richly caparisoned; he also had valuable dogs procured from various countries, of breeds not known in France.

The library contained forty thousand volumes, and was considered an institution of great merit. It is easy enough nowadays to form a library with that number of books, but then it was a great labour. The King's library, which had only ten thousand volumes, had hitherto been considered a very valuable one; and those lately founded by Bodley at Oxford, Angelo Bocca in Rome, and Boromée in Milan, were cited as rare and magnificent examples, though they could not be regarded as rivalling that in the Palais Mazarin. It was the Cardinal's own idea to make the largest collection yet known, and to open it daily to the public. Over the entrance was written the invitation, "Entrez tous qui veulent lire, entrez."[1]

Few monuments have been of more use, and excited less regret, than this act of generosity of the great Cardinal, and it is satisfactory to remember that he did not give himself over entirely to luxury, for his mind was open to better things. He loved letters, and wrote well, and he loved his books too, though he lacked time for much reading. He gave one proof of this in the care he bestowed on the bindings, and realising that bookbinding was a trade much practised in France he greatly encouraged it, which not only spoke well for his taste, but was also a politic movement.

We cannot however exonerate Mazarin from a taste for luxury. He was an ease-loving man, much occupied with his comforts and the care of his person. He enjoyed fine linen and scents and unguents; though when he first came to France he had been content with very modest surroundings, he soon was determined not only to copy Richelieu, but to eclipse him, and now he put no bridle on his extravagances.

He was able to reach the Queen's apartment through the garden by a private staircase, but even

---

[1] La Borde, *Palais Mazarin.* The library still exists, and is called "La Bibliothèque Nationale."

this short distance was too far to please Anne. She assigned a suite in the Palais Royal for the sole use of the Minister, so his magnificent mansion became a mere place of rest when he wished to be alone, and it was called the " Retiro."

Every large house in Paris at that time had a garden—that is, a parterre—laid out, but nobody sought to wander about, or be interested in watching the beauties of nature. The Cardinal's garden, however, was much more than a parterre, it was a real attempt at what we call landscape gardening, with shady groves, and banks of flowers, and pleasant retired *bosquets*.

Thus the two lovers lived in close proximity to each other, and were generally under the same roof. He had but to pass through the private passage to reach the Queen's room, and report said that he passed by that way very often.[1]

The religious party still continued their struggle against this intimacy, which was only too well known. They tried to trouble the Queen's mind by telling her her immortal soul was in danger. The Cardinal knew this was where the danger lay, and that they assailed the weakest spot in her armour.

He sought to fill her mind with other interests than those connected with pious works, and tried literature and art, hoping thus she would have fresh thoughts, and not brood over the ghostly counsels she received. But if Anne was devout, she was

[1] Le Comte Bussy-Rabutin, *Histoire en abrégée de Louis le Grand.*

even more lazy, and he made but little progress in that direction.

However, he knew her little weaknesses, her vanity of her person, her yielding nature, and he knew how to push this advantage home; he made the most of all the gifts he possessed, and his cleverness and fascination resumed their sway. Those conferences that began by being of short duration gradually grew longer and longer, and more intimate, and lasted well into the night.[1]

Anne was obstinate in many things, and tried to be resolute, but she could not withstand the siege that was laid to her heart. Though she had grown more serious and staid as time went on, she did not lose the one passion that remained steadfast and filled her whole life. Her friends even tried to involve her in fresh love affairs, but there was no room for any other love in her tender and devoted nature, and Mazarin's ascendency grew and consolidated during these years of peace before the revolutionary movement.

The pamphlets and gazetteers of the time no longer even attempted to veil the intimacy between the Queen-Regent and her Minister. In verse and in prose all sorts of ribald rhymes were scattered broadcast, some amusing, others coarse and witless.[2]

The author of the *Requeste Civile*, in writing on the subject, said, "If the rumour was true that they

[1] *Le Chartre, Coll. Petitot*, vol. ii. p. 213.
[2] *Loret, auteur des chansons obscènes les "Mazarinades."*

were bound by a marriage, ratified by the Père Vincent, then these impertinent, coarse remarks would have been long ago forgotten."

Certainly these scurrilous verses were no proof, but they are a testimony to the general opinion.

It was supposed by some that the Cardinal had married the Queen before he had taken full orders. The Princesse Palatine, who was sister to the Queen of Poland, and related to the royal family, held to this opinion, and in a letter written in 1717 she declared that Madame Beauvais, one of Anne's bed-chamber women, had been in the secret of this marriage, before Mazarin was bound by his obligations to remain a celibate; but as these allegations were made seventy years after the events, they are of little value.[1] Others gravely affirm that he never did take orders at all.[2] And others declared he never took the higher orders, but they have no proof to bring forward.[3] There is more truth in the fact that he was appointed Cardinal in 1641, and clothed with full ecclesiastical dignities,[4] and that he administered the Sacraments to his dying sister—a proof that he did receive full orders of the priesthood.[5] Moreover, Pope Urban VIII., who might easily have granted him a dispensation, would never have allowed him to

[1] *Mémoires de la Princesse Palatine*, published in Brunswick in 1789.
[2] Michelet, *M. Cheruel, Éditeur de Saint-Simon*.
[3] Aubery, *Histoire du Cardinal Mazarin*, published 1695.
[4] *Procès-verbal du Consistoire*, 1641.
[5] Daniel de Cosnac, Archevêque d'Aix, *Mémoires*, vol. i. p. 252, published by the Société de l'Histoire de France.

retain the purple and remain a Cardinal, had he been married by the rites of the Church.

It would be easy to bring many more authorities to bear, but enough has been said on this subject, which has served for a great deal of discussion, and which certainly can never be verified or cleared up.

The study of their lives seems to render all these theories an absurdity. That the union that existed between them, which may possibly have been only a union of heart and inclination, was consecrated by marriage, seems doubtful, although Mazarin's letters to the Queen, of which more hereafter, were of an ardent nature, suggesting some tie between them. But the whole tenor of their history does not point to any authorised marriage.

It was no passing sentiment, and Mazarin remained true to Anne to the end of his days. We read of no love affairs in other quarters, and his life was spent in a regular manner and without scandal. He never stood in the attitude of a husband; all their correspondence was of a passionate, anxious nature, far removed from the calm and peaceful confidence of matrimony. If Mazarin was lacking in the warm affection the Queen displayed, in a man of his nature it was not surprising that her perpetual tenderness often caused him moments of impatience; but such has ever been the end of a secret passion, generally more fervent in the heart of the woman than in that of the man.

A change was inevitable as years went on. Mazarin was a very devoted and submissive lover in the first instance, then growing bolder, and becoming full of passion, or feigning to be so. After that he needed moments of relief from the yoke he had thus put upon himself, and he became more despotic, more exacting, with his ardour gradually getting colder, while that of Anne remained ever the same.

He dominated her often by unkindness, and she trembled at his anger, and his counsels were orders to be obeyed, but on the whole their relations were peaceful.[1] A nature such as Anne's was bound to be overruled, and in obeying him she found her truest happiness.

[1] *Mémoires de l'Abbé de Choisy.*

CHAPTER XVI

GATHERING STORMS

THE Cardinal, being now suitably lodged, determined to bring some members of his family from Italy to reside with him. He had much natural affection, and had always kept up very friendly relations with his sisters.

It was accordingly arranged between them that Madame Martinozzi should send her daughter Anna Maria, and that two girls and a boy of the Mancini family should accompany their cousin.[1] These girls were all pretty, and just entering their teens; the Mancini were brunettes, while Mademoiselle de Martinozzi was fair and very handsome.

A great future lay before these children, especially the girls. The Duc d'Orleans remarked on seeing them, " All the world will gather round these little girls, and nearly smother them with attentions; they will soon have fine houses, good fortunes, jewels and plate, and probably attain to high dignities. But the boy must make his way, which will take more time, and he may never attain to the good fortune he will see dangling before his eyes,"—

---

[1] Anna Maria married eventually the Prince de Conti; Laure, the eldest of the Mancini, married the Duc de Mercœur; and Olympe, the second, married the Comte de Soissons.

meaning that the uncle might sink from his present high estate before his nephew had come to manhood. As a fact the boy died before his august relative, being killed in a combat in the Faubourg St. Antoine.[1]

When the Cardinal received word of the arrival of the children, he left the Queen and hastened to meet them in his own house. He brought them over that evening to the Palais Royal, to present them to Anne, who kissed them very affectionately and admired them greatly.[2]

The offspring of the sisters of Mazarin showed plainly the vigorous race from which he sprang, and nearly all of them gave great promise of beauty as well as glowing health. The Cardinal did not appear to pay much attention to them at first, though there is no doubt he had great designs for their future, and his indifference was assumed. The following day they again returned to court, and, as the Duc d'Orleans had remarked, were in danger of being smothered by too many attentions; but their extreme youth obliged them to be kept for a while in the background.

On Twelfth Night the Queen spent the evening in solitude; she liked the calm and peace of a few hours alone after all the many festivities of the opening year, and was quite indifferent to State receptions, or the crowds who thought it their duty to appear before her. Mazarin was supping at the

---

[1] He was killed July 2, 1651.
[2] Amédée René, *Nièces de Mazarin.*

Prince de Condé's, and all the retinue of the court had flocked there. This caused no annoyance to Anne—her one wish was that all should follow and pay court to the Minister, but to amuse the children she sent for a cake, and the ladies who were in waiting partook of the little feast, and drank their healths in hippocras. Whatever her tastes might have been in her young days, she now showed a preference for quiet home amusements.

Although the atmosphere seemed to be calm, this was far from being the case, already there was a vague murmur of discontent, and the air was charged with revolt.

A mutiny had broken out among the shop-keepers in Paris, on account of a new tax which had been laid upon them. Their numbers having increased considerably, they sought an interview with the Minister, and expressed themselves with such violence that he was completely taken aback. The Queen had been obliged to hold a Council to discuss what measures should be taken to suppress these disorders.

The princes of the blood treated the matter lightly, and did not forgo their Twelfth Night entertainment, but though the Cardinal willingly joined their parties in order to forget these troubles in feasting and gaming, he was far from easy.

The following morning, on her way to Mass, the Queen was beset by two hundred women, who followed her to the church crying out for justice. This alarmed her greatly, especially as it had been arranged that the King should attend a thanksgiving service after his late recovery; as it had been publicly announced, Anne did not dare to put it off. She let him go in fear and trembling, and ordered his guards to be doubled.

Meanwhile there were various abuses in the palace itself, which were causing comment. It was said that only the higher salaried officers of the Crown ever got paid, and that their juniors had to go without, also that the Queen had ceased to show that fine liberality for which she had been noted.

Angry comments were made, as the savings of the past year had amounted to 42 millions, there should have been no lack of money. The Cardinal was accredited with having kept back half for himself, but as the princes took their share, it was impossible he should have annexed such vast sums as was supposed. The princes were called the " thieves," the Cardinal the " Corsair," and a cry arose against the Minister. There was no doubt that he received enormous sums at the expense of the nation, and his revenues were immense. The charge of the King's education was supposed to be purely honorary, but for that he received 60,000 livres; pay of Minister, 20,000; pay of Member of Council, 6,000; pay of Cardinal, 18,000; extra pension from Queen, 110,000; and later on he had 21 abbayes, which were worth 468,330 livres.[1]

No wonder that an outcry was being made. The

[1] *Lettres d'Instructions, Mémoires de Colbert,* vol. i. p. 520, published by Clement.

perpetual assembling of the *Parlement* and deputations worried the Queen greatly ; she quite lost heart, and used to say despondently after one of these meetings, " I suppose it will all begin again to-morrow."

Once, even in the presence of the Duc d'Orleans, she became so exasperated that she showed displeasure with the Minister, and seemed to lay the blame on him. As soon as the Duke had left the room, Mazarin, who always outstayed every one else, said sternly :

" I perceive, Madame, that your Majesty is offended with me. I have not succeeded in my constant desire, which is to serve you. My head must answer for it."[1]

Poor Anne burst into tears—the anger of Mazarin was always more than she could bear ; she poured out a flood of apologies and entreaties, till at last he allowed himself to be mollified.

The deputies continued to address angry remonstrances to the Queen. The state of the finances alone rendered the situation dangerous, but Anne could not be brought to see this. She laughed at the very idea of serious trouble, and said that revolutions were not such easy things in Paris as they seemed to imagine, and that for her part she knew how to throw roses to her deputies, but that if they would not give way she knew how to punish them.[1]

The fact is, like many weak and vain persons,

[1] *Mémoires de Retz.*
[2] Avocat-Général, *Mémoires d'Omer Talon.*

she, had a great idea of her own importance, she could not be brought to see that her influence was waning, and she objected extremely to any reproaches that seemed to lessen the royal dignity.

She agreed to attend the assembly with the King, but it was remarked that the cries of " Vive le Roi " were few, and that a general chilliness pervaded the meeting.

The Minister was infinitely annoyed by this spirit of hostility, but his policy was always for moderation. He kept the Queen back as much as possible, and tried to prevent her making speeches. He was determined to hazard nothing, and, above all, not even allow the semblance of a civil war; but in spite of his prudence, trouble was inevitable.

On the great fête-day in August, 1648, the King went to attend vespers at Notre Dame, accompanied by the Cardinal. Anne had gone, according to her custom, into retreat at Val-de-Grace. Her rigid habits of devotion must often have annoyed Mazarin, that callous man of the world, who made no pretence even to so much religion as might have been expected from one of his calling. In the *Mémoires* of Madame de Motteville, there is always a strong note of disapproval of the Cardinal. It was only natural that the faithful bed-chamber woman should have viewed with hostility the lover of her mistress, although she never would admit that he actually stood in this relation, and only wrote of him with great bitterness, ignoring all statements that would sound injurious to the Queen.

The Marquis de Gesvres, Captain of the Guard, was in attendance on the King, and it was his duty to keep all outsiders from entering the cloisters while his Majesty was going in procession round them. The place was full of roughs, and they absolutely refused to go, and replied insolently to the lieutenant, M. de l'Ile, that they would not move.

De Gesvres, in this emergency, ordered his subaltern to turn them out any way he could. A riot at once ensued, and two of the guards lay dead on the ground within the sacred precincts.

It was a crime of *lèse-majesté* to draw a sword in the King's presence. A great feeling of uneasiness arose after this incident, and the Cardinal, besides, was furious because he had not been consulted first as to what measures should be taken, seeing that he was in charge of the Sovereign.[1]

Jarzé, a friend of the Provost, blamed De Gesvres for having been too prompt in his action, and so much stir was made that next morning the Marquis de Gesvres was ordered to give up his maréchal's baton. His father, the Comte de Trémes, thereupon came and complained to the Minister of the treatment meted out to his son, and the Cardinal replied that, as Minister and chief tutor to the King, no orders should have been given in his presence, and he considered that the Marquis had been entirely in the wrong.

[1] Montglat accuses the Cardinal of cowardice. He changed colour when the swords were drawn, and as every one noticed his fear he became ashamed, and revenged himself on the Marquis de Gesvres.—*Mémoires Montglat.*

In the evening, when the Queen came in from her drive, Louis ran to embrace her, and as she noticed that he was not accompanied as usual by the Captain of the Guard, she asked the reason.

It was told her that the Comte de Trémes refused to allow the Comte du Charost, who had been appointed in the place of his son, to take up the post.

"This is too much!" cried the outraged Queen. "Have things come to such a pass that it is considered an honour to disobey me?"

The Cardinal was sent for, and she ordered the four Captains of the Guard to appear—the Marquis de Villequier, the Comte de Trémes, the Comte de Charost, and the Marquis de Chandenier.

She reprimanded them all severely, but when they began to back each other up, and give their reasons, she lost her temper, and telling them that she would find others who would obey her better, she turned them out.

The court was now in an uproar; some approved of the Queen's high-handed measure, especially at a time when her authority was being disputed, others took the part of the disgraced officers.

As a rule, the kindness of Anne's heart prevented her from ever turning any one out of her household, but whether the disturbance in the air had contaminated her also, or whether she was influenced by her knowledge of the Cardinal's aversion to some of these men, she would not reconsider her decision, and thus added one more to the many grievances which his enemies had now piled up against Mazarin.

CHAPTER XVII

MAZARIN IN DANGER

IN August the news of the death of the King of Poland was received. The Queen took but little interest in this intelligence, and only felt annoyance at having to put her court in mourning. She did not care enough for his widow, on whose head she had helped to place the royal crown, to give much thought to what became of her.

The affairs at home were much more pressing, and the battle of Lens, which was won by the French army that same month, was of far greater moment. The Queen desired that a solemn Te Deum should be sung at Notre Dame as a thanksgiving to God, who had granted success to their arms, and she took advantage of this day of triumph to arrest suddenly three of the chief leaders of the opposition—Blancmesnil, Charton, and an aged councillor named Broussel. This was intended as a punishment for the *Parlement*, who had so often disobeyed her orders. Broussel was a man over sixty years of age, and had always been a somewhat violent member of the opposition.

De Cominges was charged with the carrying out of this arrest—no easy matter, as Broussel was the idol of the people. He went in his own carriage with four of his guards to the Rue Saint Landry, where the old councillor lived. It was so narrow that they were obliged to get out of the vehicle and proceed on foot.

The officer in charge knocked at the door of the house, and a little page opened it. They at once seized the entrance, and going in found Broussel seated with his family at dinner. De Cominges showed the order for his arrest, signed in the King's name, and desired him to come at once, and without resistance.

Broussel at first replied that he was ill and unable to comply, and then asked leave to be at least allowed to dress decently, as he was only in a dressing-gown and slippers.

While they were parleying an old woman in the house raised an alarm, crying out for help, and loading the men with shrill abuse The neighbours came running out, and when they saw a coach with soldiers and arms they were filled with rage, and rushed to the rescue: some wanted to cut the harness, others to smash the carriage. The officer, seeing that there was no time to lose, threatened Broussel with instant death if he lingered, and tearing him from the arms of his relations, hurried him to the coach.

But the rescuers had been before him, and he found that chains had been thrown across the streets, so that he had to turn back and double in all directions. The intrepid De Cominges would hardly have succeeded in carrying off his prisoner, his coach being overturned, if he had not met a company of his own guards, who came to his assistance. They seized upon a passing coach full of ladies, and, in spite of their remonstrances, turned them out and put Broussel into it, and obliged the coachman to drive on, while the populace wrecked the vehicle of De Cominges as the only vengeance in their power.[1]

Even this tumult did not rouse those at court to the imminent danger. Anne did not understand the situation, and Mazarin scorned the idea of peril. Consternation prevailed all the same.

"If Mazarin does not take care," said the Prince de Condé, "he will ruin the State," and indeed it looked like it at that moment.

When the morrow broke there were no signs of peace, rather had the tumult increased. The Chancellor Lequier fled for his life to the palace. The people wished to seize him, crying out, "It will be prisoner for prisoner, and we can make an exchange." Others more brutal said, "No, rather let us tear him limb from limb."

When the Queen awoke on the second morning, this was the news that was brought to her, as well as the report that the *Parlement* were sending a deputation to claim the release of the prisoner, so that she had to rise and dress at once.

The palace at this time was full of company, including the English Queen. Mazarin looked

[1] *Mémoires de Brienne, Coll. Petitot.*

calm as ever, and displayed neither fear nor anxiety. He attended the meeting as usual, placed at the Queen's side. It took place in the small gallery, and was an informal affair. Anne was extremely indignant, and blamed the chief magistrates in no measured terms. "The King my son will one day learn what happened, and will punish you severely."

The Cardinal spoke much more moderately, and said that doubtless the prisoners would be released if they would engage not to interfere in public affairs.[1] The Cardinal de Retz advised the Queen "to give up the old rascal dead or alive, to restore him dead might not be in accordance with her piety or prudence, but to restore him alive would quell the tumult."[2]

In the end Anne was unwillingly obliged to give way. It was an humiliation for her, her Minister, and all such persons as cared for the honour of France.

The members of the *Parlement* departed from the Palais Royal in triumph. Crowds were waiting to know the result, and they replied that they had received a promise for the release of Broussel; but so great was the rage and indignation against the Queen and Cardinal that the people did not hesitate to declare that, should the promise be broken, they would sack the palace, and turn out the insolent foreigner who ruled the affairs of the

[1] *Mémoires d'Omer Talon.*
[2] *Mémoires du Cardinal de Retz.*

nation, and cries arose of "Long live the King, but no one else save Broussel." It might have been thought when Broussel had been released that all the rioting would subside, but one set of malcontents after another kept up the flames and riots in the Rue Saint-Honoré and the Rue Saint-Antoine, filling even the mocking courtiers with alarm, and fears were entertained that the palace would be set on fire.

The horrible peril she was in was brought forcibly before the Queen by Jarzé, the new Captain of Guard. With some ostentation he said,

"Madame, we are but a handful of men here, but we will die at our post."

Mazarin at this crisis seemed paralysed with fear, and gave the Queen no comfort, but though the words of Jarzé struck a chill to her heart, she showed laudable calmness, and with a courage worthy of a granddaughter of the valiant Charles V., she replied,

"Do not fear. God will protect the innocent King; let us put our trust in Him."[1]

She remained all the following night ready in case of an alarm, while Mazarin abandoned his violet robes for a grey suit, as at any moment he might be obliged to flee, and his horses were kept saddled all night.

But by degrees the mob scattered in all directions, in that extraordinary way in which crowds melt away without any apparent reason for it; the

[1] *Mémoires de Motteville.*

people returned to their own homes, and for this time at least Paris was saved.

The Queen's nerves, however, were sadly shaken. On September 12 she announced her intention of going to Rueil for a few days, giving as her reason that the Palais Royal was in such a filthy condition that it was necessary to put it in the hands of the cleaners.

The people had shown openly their distrust of the King being removed from Paris, and the Cardinal had been so loaded with imprecations that he did not even dare return to his own house. Only the Queen drove abroad and showed herself incessantly; but she longed all the more for the peace and safety of country life, and on the pretext above named made her preparations to leave.

The following morning at six o'clock the King, accompanied by the Cardinal, drove out before Paris had awakened from its slumbers. At the town gates some idlers who recognised them raised a cry of "Aux armes," and tried to stop the royal coach, but they were not in sufficient numbers to do any mischief. The Queen had remained behind with "petit Monsieur," so as to give colour to the idea that their departure was a matter of no moment.

The Cardinal, who was anxious about her, sent back a messenger begging her to follow with as little delay as possible; but with far more courage than he displayed, and without changing any of her arrangements, she bade her little boy good-bye (he was recovering from the small-pox) and drove off to see her friends the nuns at Val-de-Grace. From there she went to the Hôtel de Ville, to give an audience to the Provost of the Markets, and then quietly gave the order to proceed to Rueil.[1]

There was really nothing extraordinary in removing the court from Paris at that season; but the people were in such an irritable condition it was hard to say what they might not resent; once safely away, however, neither the Queen nor the Cardinal had any desire to return. When it was proposed that the latter should do so, he objected, and said it would be against the wishes of the Duc d'Orleans; this subterfuge did not impose on any one, certainly not on the Duke, who laughed at it with scorn.

The court did not return to Paris till the approach of winter obliged them to do so.

[1] *Mémoires de Brienne.*

CHAPTER XVIII

THE FRONDE

ONCE more a new year was begun, and the fête of Twelfth Night, which was held with so much festivity in France, was destined, in 1649, to be fraught with great consequences.

Anne had held a secret council, at which it was decided that the King and Queen should leave Paris, for the only way to reduce the magistrates, the insurgents, and the populace to order was to blockade the capital. The 6th of January was the day fixed on.

The Queen spent the evening in playing a game with the King, her ladies standing round watching it—in those court circles people found their amusement in doing nothing at all—when one of them, Madame de la Tremouille, was ill-advised enough to whisper,

" There is a rumour in Paris that the Queen is leaving to-night."

Anne either did not hear or paid no attention. She helped the King to cut up the cake, asking her ladies to take slices, while one was set aside for the Virgin.[1] That one slice contained the bean,

[1] *Mémoires de Motteville*, vol. ii.

and as there was no claimant for it, Anne was proclaimed " Reine de la Fève."

These innocent amusements were continued into the night, and a joke was raised about her Majesty's proposed departure, which was treated as absurd.

Just before she retired for the night her equerry Beringhen came in, she took him aside, and in a whisper ordered the King's carriage to be got ready.

After midnight she rose from her seat, and informed her ladies that she was going to speak to the Minister about an important charity. As they afterwards remarked, this might have opened their eyes to the fact that something unusual was going on, for she was not in the habit of explaining her actions to them.

After the consultation was over—it was but a few hurried words—the Queen undressed and got into bed. Meanwhile Mademoiselle de Beaumont, who had come in from supping with Beringhen, gave it as her opinion to the others that some design was on foot, and that it was no joking matter.

When all was quiet in the palace, Anne rose, assisted by the waiting-woman on duty in the royal bed-chamber. At three in the morning the King and " petit Monsieur" were roused and carried down to where the carriages were waiting in the great courtyard.

The Cardinal had spent the evening supping with the Duc d'Orleans, to allay suspicion; but he too had laid his plans, and his household were even then engaged in packing up his valuables, and removing his nieces to the care of Madame de Senacé.

It was dark and cold, a bitter winter night. The Queen, followed by her woman, had slipped down the little private staircase that led from her room to the garden—only one small lantern guided her stumbling steps—and joined her sons in the courtyard. Considering the number of people concerned in the enterprise, the secret had been well kept.

The Captains of the Guards and her principal ladies were in waiting. The Princes of the blood, with Madame and Mademoiselle d'Orleans, and the Princesses de Condé were grouped together; these with their attendants made a large party. The friends and relations about to depart clung together so as to seek safety with those they loved, for Paris at daybreak was to be made to suffer for the King's displeasure towards his capital. The Cardinal was in attendance, his followers were assembled in large numbers, feeling, and with truth, that for them there was no safety save in flight.

The Queen courageously made light of this midnight journey, declaring that eight days would see them back, and mounted into her coach with the King and the Minister, wrapped in furs against the inclemency of the weather. "Petit Monsieur" was in another carriage with his attendants. The great gates were opened, and the heavy coaches rolled out into the deserted streets.

But if she looked on it as a picnic, it was going to prove a very uncomfortable one.

When the royal party reached St. Germain-en-Laye, they found themselves in an empty palace, without beds, or furniture, or plate, or linen, and also without any household, as it was always the custom when the court moved to bring all necessaries with them.

The Cardinal had had the forethought to send out two little camp-beds a few days previously. Into these the Queen and the royal children crept, chilled to the bone, to take a few hours of restless slumber.

The Duchesse d'Orleans slept on a pile of straw, and Mademoiselle did the same. All who had followed the court had no better couches either, and in a few hours straw had become so valuable in St. Germain that it was not to be got for love or money.[1]

When it was known at daybreak that the King and Queen-Regent had left Paris the greatest consternation prevailed. They had both left letters for the Deputies, declaring that they wished no harm to their people, but the state of things was such that they could no longer reside in their capital in safety. Those of their adherents who had remained in Paris were in hourly dread of pillage, and not without cause, for the houses of the nobles were shortly searched, and many fled disguised as women; but they had so many grievous adventures

[1] *Mémoires de Brienne.*

before they reached St. Germain, they might almost better have remained.

Meanwhile the King's army was ordered to blockade the city, and seize all the provisions that were brought in from the country; the idea was that a week at the very most of this treatment would bring the Parisians to their senses. But they had greatly miscalculated the strength of the insurgents.

The party led by the Duc de Bouillon against the King's troops received the title of La Fronde.[1] The Prince de Conti was declared generalissimo of the army of La Fronde, and, accompanied by his sister, Madame de Longueville, they having both openly thrown off allegiance to the royal cause, repaired to the Hôtel de Ville, where they were joined by the Duchesse de Bouillon.

These ladies were both very beautiful; they stood on the steps outside the building, each holding in her arms a lovely child, and declaring they were hostages in the hands of the people. The crowds, which not only filled the streets, but swarmed upon the house-tops, received them with enthusiasm, they

[1] The origin of this name arose from an exercise employed by the volunteers for amusement in the ditches outside Paris, of throwing stones with slings called "frondes." In the assembly one day the son of one of the councillors, who was in opposition to his father, said, "Quand ce sera à mon tour, je fronderai bien l'opinion de mon père." Being a play on the word, which had a double meaning, and was sometimes used for censure or taunt. This made his hearers laugh, and after that all those in opposition to the court party were called *frondeurs*. The word was taken up, the shop-keepers seized upon it, and hats, ribbons, gloves, and fans were called "A la mode de la Fronde."—*Mémoires de Montglat and De Retz.*

and their husbands being greeted as saviours of the people.

Madame de Longueville was constituted Queen by the *frondeurs*, and her court was singularly free from etiquette, for the greatest freedom prevailed. The most violent declamations against the Queen and Cardinal were to be heard, and the licentious young officers flocked in numbers to offer their homage to the beautiful Duchess.[1]

On January 21 the generals of the Fronde made a grand sortie, with the view to bringing in a convoy of wheat, which, however, they could not find, and brought nothing back from this great military exploit but violent colds, as the weather was bitter. Bread had begun to rise in price, and anger against any persons suspected of being *Mazarins* was very violent.

Even the servants of the palace were maltreated, and the King's furniture and even his clothes were seized.

Meanwhile the nobles at St. Germains were in a sad plight. Their numbers had greatly increased, which added to the difficulty of providing for them. They had no furniture but what the soldiers of the royal army were able to procure by ransacking the villages in the neighbourhood.

The Duc d'Orleans was extremely annoyed at the part his brother, the Prince de Conti, had taken, as well as his sister, Madame de Longueville. De Conti was neither physically nor mentally fit for the

[1] *Mémoires de Brienne.*

task he had undertaken; he was hump-backed, and had never been considered to have much sense, and his brother was therefore doubly annoyed at the position he had been placed in.[1]

Once more the *frondeurs* sent out their army, but it really consisted of the lowest rabble of Paris, and the Prince de Conti could do nothing with them. It was a strange state of things—a besieged town supported by the *Parlement*, and no one very certain as to who could be trusted.

The Duc d'Orleans sent the deputies a letter of explanation, saying he felt it his duty to remain by the King and Queen, but that he was filled with grief at the siege of Paris, and advised peace.

Mazarin, knowing the hatred in which he was held, announced that he thought it would be well if he left France, as long as the royal prestige would not be hurt by his doing so.

Some one said mockingly to him that all would go well if he would only depart, upon which he replied in all seriousness that he was ready to go if only he could see the King obeyed and respected by his people. There were not wanting some in authority who counselled the Queen to dismiss Mazarin; but while such advice was against the dictates of her own heart, she also declared she had no one to put in his place.

---

[1] "Le Prince de Conti etait bossu et contrefait tellement, que le Prince de Condé passant par la chambre du Roi saluat fort humblement un singe qui etait attaché a un chenet de la cheminée disant avec derision, 'Serviteur au generalissimo des Parisiens.'"
—*Mémoires de Montglat.*

The Cardinal was always in negotiation with people inside Paris, either treating with his enemies, or with those who, hating him, yet thought it advisable not to quarrel with him altogether. In this he resembled Catherine de' Medici, who to gain time made peace with the Huguenots more than once.

The two armies continued to face each other, without doing much harm on either side. That of the King had done all that it intended to do; that of Paris was too feeble to attack, and, lacking in courage as well, remained in the Place Royale.[1]

The Duc de Beaufort made one more attempt to seize a convoy of wheat and oxen, which were sorely needed, and this time he was successful. He risked his own life in the enterprise, and when it was known that he was returning with his spoils such crowds went out to meet him that the whole night was spent, and part of the next day, in trying to get the animals through the dense throng, which was one struggling mass of men and beasts.

On February 12 a Herald-at-Arms on the part of the King arrived at the gate of St. Honoré. But the Captain of the Guard refused him admittance unless he had a pass from the Prince de Conti.[2] The Queen, hearing of the distress among the poor, sold some valuable earrings, and ordered the

---

[1] The Prince de Conti held reviews in the Place Royale in presence of the ladies, who greatly admired the troops, as they were very gay, the soldiers adorned with ribbons.—*Mémoires de Montglat.*

[2] The Cardinal suggests that this was really a trap on the part of Mazarin, and not an overture for peace.—*Mémoires de Retz.*

money to be distributed among the starving populace: in return they loaded her with imprecations.

While these horrors were going on, far worse ones were happening across the Channel, where the luckless King of England, Charles I., had met his fate on the scaffold. It almost seemed as if divine justice was threatening all the courts of Europe, not even sparing the unfortunate or innocent. His unhappy wife was bowed down with grief when the news was brought to her, living as she was in the midst of the miseries in her own native country.

Deputation after deputation went between Paris and St. Germain, without coming to any determination on either side; but still the cry of the people was, "No peace. No Mazarin. We will fetch back our good King and throw the *Mazarins* into the river." Against such feelings the wisest and most moderate were powerless.

But when things had got to this pass, news arrived which humbled the pride of the Parisians. The King's army would shortly be augmented by Vicomte de Turenne's battalions returning from Germany, and the tide of war seemed about to turn. The generals of the Fronde now saw fit to enter into a treaty. Their troops had proved themselves of little account, and all their remonstrances had failed to remove the hated Italian.

Moreover, certain people even in the opposition were in favour of his remaining—the nobles to whom he offered preferment, and the courtiers who found it to their interest to keep in with him. His own Cabinet detested him, and it was the fashion in France to abuse him; all the same, opinion was divided as to whether it would be wise altogether to expel him.

The *Parlement* made one last effort to raise difficulties about signing the peace should the Minister remain, but they had to give in.

Peace was signed on March 11, and the court returned to Paris. Thus ended this extraordinary campaign, almost without parallel in history. A king in exile in his own country, besieging his own capital. The royal princes in the ranks of the besieged and besiegers. People famished in the streets of Paris, and the royal family, living in squalor and misery in their own country residence. And all this was practically the work of Mazarin; the Fronde would never have existed but for him.

This insurrection will go down to posterity coupled with the name of the all-powerful Italian Cardinal, who, while apparently in submission to the King his master, in reality sat side by side with Anne of Austria on the throne of France.

CHAPTER XIX

THE AFFAIR OF THE MARQUIS DE JARZÉ

THE Duc d'Orleans was the first to return to Paris. Anne waited a few days at St. Germain, and received Madame de Longueville with great coldness when that lady had the effrontery to come from Paris to visit her, and when the Court did return to the Palais Royal things had not greatly improved.

It is true that the King was warmly welcomed, for in those days his presence in their midst had a great charm for the Parisians. He was useful to them, and added to the prestige of the capital. Through all the wars and seditions, their one real fear was to lose their Monarch, consequently the *frondeurs* had dreaded nothing so much as his return, knowing the hold he had over the hearts of the people.

The country at large was in a state of ferment, and the finances in a critical condition in the provinces, even the King's household was in a pitiable state. The palace was badly kept and the table very poor, the question of the salaries of the subordinates was still causing great discord, and the gentlemen of the court were sending away their pages, not having sufficient means to keep them. The army was unpaid, and the crown jewels had been pawned. In fact, affairs were desperate, and the monarchy, once so great and opulent, whose King and court had been the admiration of all Europe, was in these few short months reduced to penury. When Charles II., King of England, though still a fugitive, arrived in France, be was received with royal honours, but the entertainment which Louis gave to welcome him was meagre in the extreme. It was stately by reason of the royal persons assembled at the board, but it could hardly be dignified by the name of a banquet.

The English court was lodged at St. Germain, and judging by the accounts lately given of that palace, the guests were not in the lap of luxury. Few French nobles visited them, and it is not surprising that the English lords who had followed the fortunes of their Prince, complained bitterly of their solitude and discomfort.

The Duc de Vendôme now thought fit to make up his quarrel with the Cardinal, and as a token of his goodwill proposed a marriage between his son, the Duc de Mercœur, and the eldest of the Mancini girls.[1]

Mazarin neither accepted nor refused. It was an alliance to his advantage, and with the wealth he could give was by no means a bad one for the Duke; but the Cardinal never allowed his hand to

---

[1] Bazin de Raucon, *Histoire de France sous le Ministère de Mazarin.*

be forced, or accepted too eagerly what might be only a bait.

His nieces were growing in beauty and charm day by day, which did not, however, prevent their being satirised in the many verses published at the time.

Anne was now settled in Paris with her children; the King was growing fast, and her second boy had been taken away from his nurses, and given a household of his own, with his full title of Monsieur.

As soon as the Duchesse de Chevreuse, who was in Brussels, heard of the general peace, she hastened to Paris and joined her husband and daughter. She had received a sort of pardon, and a promise from the Cardinal that she might present herself at court; but Mazarin had no intention of letting her down too gently, and he advised Anne to refuse the request of the Duc de Chevreuse, that his wife might remain there permanently.

The Queen was of the same opinion, and replied that she could not risk allowing a woman who had not been true to her, to reside in a city so full of cabals and enemies, unless she showed absolute submission.

The old Duke, who was 84 years of age, and very deaf, answered that he would guarantee the good conduct of his wife, but the Queen responded that he never had, and never would have, any power whatever to restrain her.

Mademoiselle de Chevreuse had grown very pretty, with eyes which alone ensured her having many conquests. She had good features, but was rather too sallow and thin for real beauty. With such a mother, it is hardly surprising to hear that she was frivolous in the extreme. She was supremely silly, often bordering on the ridiculous. She treated her lovers as if they were so much discarded finery; but her position was an advantageous one, and she did not lack suitors. As she was free to come or go from France, she had long ago returned to join her father.[1]

When Madame de Chevreuse arrived the court was at Compiégne, and it was there she paid her first visit to the Queen. She had been ill, and was pale and dejected, and quite ready to take up the submissive part dictated to her; weary of exile, she was glad to be received back on any terms.

Anne had always been in the habit of embracing her favourite, she as a rule never kissed any of her ladies, save the Duchesse d'Orleans and Mademoiselle, who were her relatives, but this time she greeted the repentant Duchess with no such mark of affection. She listened silently to Madame de Chevreuse's promises of amendment, with a cold manner, very different from the old days.

The Duchess then bowed to the King, said a few words to the Minister, and retired.

As soon as she had left the audience chamber the Queen exclaimed,

"Why, that is not Madame de Chevreuse! She is an absolutely different person, and as changed as I am in my feelings towards her."

Whether she alluded to her loss of beauty or her

[1] *Mémoires de Retz.*

extreme humility remained a doubt to her hearers. Probably a little of both.

The Queen of Poland, at the end of her year of widowhood, married her brother-in-law, who was heir to the throne. As they were within the prohibited degree, it was necessary to get a dispensation, which was easily done. In spite of the Queen's want of youth, the marriage was approved of in Poland, and the fair Marie wrote to her friends at the French court, and told them she had been carried in triumph on a silver car to the church, and that she was extremely pleased with her new husband.

Amongst the followers of the Cardinal was the Marquis de Jarzé, or Jarsai,[1] who was witty and amusing, but had a very free tongue, and spared no one in his trenchant remarks.[2]

He used to play the Italian game of *bauchette* or bowls with Mazarin, and greatly ingratiated himself with the Cardinal, not only by being a pleasant companion, but from his readiness to plunge into every dispute, and then turn the affair into ridicule.

A feud was raging between the Duc de Beaufort and his adherents and a party of courtiers, of whom Jarzé was one.

On one occasion these gentlemen were going to Paris for some races while the court was out of town, and when they went to make their obeisance to the Queen before leaving, Jarzé, who was not

---

[1] *Mémoires de Brienne.*
[2] *Mémoires de Montglat.*

the wisest of men, turned smilingly to her, and said that they intended to hold their own against the other faction.

" For God's sake, gentlemen," replied the Queen, " I beg of you all to be prudent, and commit no rash actions."

The general place of rendezvous and amusement in Paris, especially during the races, was at the Jardin Renard. Jarzé was in the habit of holding orgies there, when he would drink to the health of Mazarin.

One afternoon during their stay, he and his comrades met in the famous gardens the Duc de Beaufort, accompanied by the Duc de Retz and others. Possibly these gentlemen did not care to encounter the *Mazarins*, for they turned into another alley, and Jarzé and his friends at once began to taunt them, crying aloud that he and his had remained masters of the field, as the *Frondeurs* dared not face the *Mazarins*. Thinking it a great joke, Jarzé repeated the story in the salons among the ladies, doubtless with amplifications, and it was at once repeated to the Duc de Beaufort. In the evening they returned to sup on the terrace at the Jardin Renard.

While so engaged the Duke appeared with a large company fully armed. The supper party saw at once that the evening was not likely to go off peacefully, but thought it best to pay no attention, and continued their repast; but De Beaufort had no intention of leaving them alone, and came up to the table. Jarzé and Ruvigny rose, and bowed respectfully.

"You sup early, gentlemen," said the Duke, and seizing the corner of the cloth he dragged it rudely off the table, the dishes falling on the ground, and the company being bespattered with the sauces and wines.

In a moment the place was in an uproar, the pages set upon Jarzé, and maltreated him, and the Duc de Candale, cousin of De Beaufort, drew his sword and attacked the others; such riots, often terminating in bloodshed, were, however, usual enough, and after a while the combatants desisted and retired.

The Queen was much annoyed when she heard of the encounter, as it was entirely a matter of party spirit, showing the ill-feeling that still continued. Nothing daunted, Jarzé determined to keep in the good graces of the Minister, and got into the habit of coming constantly to visit the Queen of an evening, and by adroit flattery and exaggerated devotion tried to prove to her that his fidelity passed even the bounds of that which is expected between a sovereign and a subject.[1]

Anne was always amused by him, and used to turn his attentions into ridicule; but the scandal-mongers, always ready with eyes and ears open, began to make much of this folly. The fact was, Jarzé was playing a double part; he was literally a spy in the palace, and used to retail all that

[1] *Mémoires de Motteville*, vol. i.

was said in private to the Prince de Condé, determined to belong to both parties, and keep in with the one which served him best.

Madame de Beauvais, the first bed-chamber woman, who was neither young nor beautiful, had fallen in love with Jarzé, and while making every use of this circumstance to increase his intimacy with Anne, he managed to throw dust in the eyes of the enamoured waiting-woman as well, and continued to show the Queen by every means in his power the stifled flame which consumed his heart, and the intense adoration for her person which was driving him mad.

Meanwhile all these rumours had been brought to the ears of the Cardinal, who began to suffer from a pretty acute attack of jealousy, almost the first intimation we have had that Mazarin was not cold-blooded after all, and could ill brook a rival. Anyway, it caused him great irritation, and he wrote in his copious notes these words, "Garsé est isy, Le Chasser," a laconic statement, but a proof of his strong objection to the man.[1]

The claims of Jarzé were ridiculous; but Anne's vanity was flattered, and though she tried to laugh it off she was a good deal pleased, and showed it.

Upon which Mazarin determined that Jarzé should be promptly ruined. First he declared that he had taken a great dislike to Madame de Beauvais, and said she must be sent away from court. Anne remonstrated, and answered that she

[1] *No.* 12, *Fonds Baluze*, p. 24.

did not keep her for the beauty of her person, or her mind, but she had very clever fingers, and excelled in the duties required of her.

"My women tell me all sorts of nonsense," she pleaded. "All this folly about Catau [her nick-name for Jarzé] goes in at one ear and out at the other, I don't really remember the half of it. She is, I assure you, quite innocent of the part attributed to her; why should I be put to the annoyance of sending her away?"

But the pleadings were in vain. Mazarin was adamant, and as usual Anne had to give way. Next morning, before setting out upon one of her usual visits to a convent, she sent for her house steward, and told him to give Madame de Beauvais notice to leave the palace, with her husband and children, and hand over the keys to him.

When he appeared before the waiting-woman with this news she was aghast. She had just been dressing the Queen, who had treated her as usual, and was quite unprepared for dismissal; she resisted for some time, but was at last advised by her friends to give in quietly.[1]

Though Jarzé knew by the disgrace meted out to his friend what was in store for himself, he went about with an air of indifference, bragging as usual.

Three days after Madame de Beauvais had been sent away, the Queen, who was perfectly furious

---

[1] Madame de Beaufort returned to office a year after. *Mémoires de Montglat, Coll. Petitot*, p. 203.

at what had happened, returning to her rooms through the long gallery, came upon Jarzé dressed and powdered, and looking his best, forming one of the line of bowing courtiers through which she had to pass; and then, as was the custom, they formed behind her, and followed her to the "Salon des Miroirs," where she did her hair.

Anne beckoned him towards her, and in a clear voice before them all said distinctly,

" Really, Monsieur Jarzé, you are too ridiculous. They tell me that you play the lover! You are a fine gallant indeed! You fill me with pity, for you should be sent to a lunatic asylum. However, I suppose one must not be hard on you, for you inherit this folly, I believe your grandfather was expelled from court, for making love to Marie de' Medici."[1]

Poor Jarzé was much taken aback at these mocking and bitter words, his self-conceit had received a severe blow, and he left the room pale and stammering. The news of his disgrace flew round like wild-fire, and the Queen by no means escaped censure. It was thought that she had behaved very badly to one she had taken up and flattered, and that his misguided affection should have been treated with silent contempt, not openly flouted, which did not add to the dignity of the Crown.

The consequences of this incident were graver than might have been imagined. The Prince de

[1] Aubeny and Chapel, *Journal inédit de Dubusson.*

Condé took Jarzé's part, and carried him off to his country place. He then announced to all who would listen that Jarzé had acted in his interests all along, while apparently a follower of the Cardinal. He twitted the Queen with her supposed love affairs, to which she retorted that she had openly expressed her ignorance of Jarzé's absurd pretensions. But all such remarks on her part did but provoke a smile, the partisans on the side of the Princes looked on with joy, seeing a possible defeat for the Minister, and the relations between the latter and the Princes became more strained than ever.

CHAPTER XX

DISAFFECTION AT COURT

THE King had not yet attended a council, and it was arranged that it should take place without loss of time, the Minister thinking it might bring the seditious party to reason. He was still in full power, all foreign affairs in his hands; but all the same he was very nervous as to his reception by the people, and there were those who said that if they gave him no special greeting he was ruined. But in such matters Mazarin was not wanting in courage and decision; if he could make himself feared, he could also make himself beloved. When the crowds gathered round the King's carriage with every sign of rejoicing, as if the rebellion had been but an evil dream, there were many scowling faces turned towards the Minister, but at the sight of that commanding presence and eagle eye the malcontents dared not openly show their hatred of him. Mazarin stood by the door of the coach, looking calmly on the multitude, and the low murmur of discontent died away, the power of the man was such that the very sight of him disarmed his foes.

If it was a demonstration in favour of the King, it soon became one in favour of the Minister. The fickle crowd began to pass remarks on his personal beauty, and some went so far as to offer him their hands. Soon they were evoking blessings on his head for having brought them back their King, and declaring that they had been mistaken, and the Cardinal was an honest man after all. Anne was in raptures, she had not ventured to hope for such a reception for her beloved Mazarin. When the ceremony was over they met with joy, congratulating each other, for both had greatly dreaded what this day might bring about.

She spent the evening with her ladies, holding forth to them on all the flattering things the washerwomen, sellers of old clothes, and women of the Halles had shouted from among the crowd in praise of the Cardinal.

When the King, a few days later, went in state to the Church of the Jesuits, beautifully dressed, and looking his best, that he might give pleasure to his subjects, Mazarin, emboldened by his late successes, went out an hour before Louis, attended only by a couple of bishops, and drove through the town to await his Majesty's arrival at the church. All fears on his account were now at an end, and with a smiling countenance he held the reins of government more firmly than ever.

Though Madame de Longueville was received on the same terms as before, she never left off her intrigues, and had ceased to be a *persona grata* with the court. This high-born lady, who had earned a reputation of extreme propriety, had lately changed her tactics, and thought her talents best bestowed on politics. She was naturally clever, besides possessing the feminine gift of a languorous beauty which charmed all who came in contact with her; but from having been the heroine of a party, she was in the end doomed to sink into being a mere adventuress.[1]

At this period she was still occupied in fermenting quarrels among the conflicting parties, she made the proposed marriage of the Duc de Mercœur with Mademoiselle Mancini a pretext to inflame the princes further against Mazarin.

The Duc de Vendôme, who had no wish to ally himself with the Cardinal unless he saw favour and preferment likely to arise from it, now began to hold back, and told Mazarin coolly that he did not see how he could even think of such a thing, so once more the affairs remained in abeyance. His niece was still so young that the Cardinal felt there was no real hurry, and was indifferent at the delay.

Madame de Longueville, however, found plenty of things with which to occupy her mischievous spirit; she now raised a fresh storm by a request that the Princesse de Marsillac should have a *tabouret*, and a right of entrance for her carriage into the Louvre.[2] The wife of the Prince de

---

[1] *Mémoires de Retz.*

[2] This question of the *tabourets*, which put the whole court into a ferment of excitement, was simply neither more nor less than that of elevating to the rank of princesses those who hitherto had not had the right to sit in the Queen's presence. This privilege had only been granted to the wives of princes of the blood, of royal bastards of France, and of the princes of Lorraine and Savoy.—*Mémoires de Motteville*, vol. iii.

Marsillac had no claim whatever to such rank. The Prince was not of royal lineage, it was but a title he bore as son of the Duc de la Rochefoucauld, who was still alive. There had, however, no doubt been instances when the privilege had been granted.

Madame de Senacé, for instance, who claimed descent for her children from the house of Foix, had succeeded in obtaining a *tabouret* for her daughter, the Comtesse de Fleix; this honour, which elevated her above the heads of many who considered her of inferior rank to themselves, opened up the question, and there was much angry discussion about it, many putting in a better claim than hers.

Madame de Longueville also had a friend, Madame de Pons, who pretended to be descended from the family d'Albret, and who demanded a *tabouret* on the plea of her exalted ancestors. Backed up by the Abbé de la Riviére, both these ladies had succeeded in obtaining the coveted dignity.

The Queen had granted these requests most unwillingly, but hoped thereby to cement the peace more firmly; Mazarin, too, was glad to see an enemy or two the less among the ranks of the court beauties.

But the dukes and marshals of France rose up with one accord, and, while not complaining of the honour granted, demanded a similar treatment for their wives and children. As the Queen detested both Madame de Longueville and Madame de Pons, and was indifferent to Madame de Marsillac, she felt free from any personal influence in the matter, and listened to the complaints of the gentlemen, only feeling disappointed that, far from bringing peace, her unfortunate appointments were causing a great deal of discord. When they were gone she turned to the Chevalier de Jars and said peevishly that people were always crying out about something or other, but that this little storm would subside as others had done. Therein she was mistaken. An assembly of the nobles was formed sufficiently powerful to annul the new *tabourets*, and many joined it; they went in a large body to see the Queen, who received them in her private apartments.

When she saw this gathering, many of whom were personal friends of her own, she knew not what to say, and the suppliants began to think, from her hesitation, that she would revoke her order—which delighted all the mischievous spirits.

But the matter was not going to be allowed to drop so easily. Next day the disaffected nobles met again, to think of some new method, and eight of their number went to visit the Duc d'Orleans to try to enlist his sympathies on their behalf. Among these were members of some of the highest families in France.

The Duke gave them little satisfaction, and said he could do nothing, and that it was the work of the Queen and the Prince de Condé. They then went to visit this latter prince, who received them very coldly, and said it was arranged entirely between the Queen and the Duc d'Orleans.

They were thus bandied about from one to the other.

The absurdity of the whole proceeding strikes one very forcibly nowadays, but it really was a burning question then. The elevation of Madame de Pons was more than they could bear, and the princes of the blood were willing to join with the nobles, if by so doing they could prevent that audacious lady at any rate from holding such undeserved honours.

But the ladies in question had no idea of giving back that, which they had managed to obtain. The husband of the one, and M. de Moissens, the brother-in-law of the other, made every effort to defend their rights.

The assembly of aggrieved nobles went once more to the Queen, and complained bitterly of the misdirected honours which she had dealt out. Another source of annoyance to them was that two other ladies, Mademoiselle de Montbazon and Madame de la Tremouille, had been granted *tabourets*. Even the grandeur of the House of Rohan, of which Mademoiselle de Montbazon was a member, gave her no real right to the distinction, while in the case of Madame de la Tremouille it had been promised to her daughters as well.

Anne in despair sent to her bishops to settle this difficult matter for her, and they harangued the deputation, advising them to be satisfied with the Queen's promises, to do as far as possible what they required, and to obey her orders with submission.

This did not satisfy the nobility at all; the dukes of France now joined their numbers, and the Queen was beginning to become extremely uneasy as to how it all would end. The *tabouret* would cease to be a privilege if every one had a right to it, and the granting of it was becoming a farce.

In the end, however, she had to give way. She revoked the privilege she had granted to Madame de Marsillac and Madame de Pons, and this in itself was a humiliating thing for her to do; but she begged to retain that given to the Comtesse de Fleix, as not only was she by birth of the royal house of Foix, but it was also given in consideration of her mother's services.

More deputations and more harangues took place, and the Queen was formally requested to ratify her promises in writing. When this at last had been obtained the nobles humbly thanked her Majesty for her kind reconsideration (which had been entirely brought about by their bullying); they also expressed their thanks to the clergy, and to the Minister, at whose house most of the meetings had been held.

The only point that remained unsettled was the *tabouret* of Mademoiselle de Montbazon, and Madame de Longueville, who hated her, was insistent that she should be deprived of it. It was a difficult matter to settle, for the daughters of the

House of Rohan had had that honour since the days of Henri IV.

The Princesse de Guémenée on her marriage with the eldest son of the Duc de Montbazon, who, as well as herself, was of the House of Rohan, had continued to hold her *tabouret*, though she was neither a royal princess nor a duchess. This prerogative had been granted by Marie de' Medici, who had never given distinctions lightly.

The Princess chose to consider that her sister-in-law, Mademoiselle de Montbazon, being equally a Rohan through her father, had the same right also, and warmly espoused her cause. The Princesse de Guémenée was a very great lady both by birth and position, and when she announced that if the request was not granted she would share her *tabouret* with her sister-in-law, it was felt that matters had indeed become very involved. The Queen was obliged to descend to subterfuge, and to promise the Princess secretly that if she would give in now about Mademoiselle de Montbazon, her own daughter should hold the coveted honour in days to come. So ended this extraordinary quarrel, which was as insignificant as it was foolish, and which certainly concluded in a manner reflecting no credit on any one concerned.

CHAPTER XXI

THE YOUNG FRONDE—RESIGNATION OF MAZARIN

NEW difficulties beset the Government from the dictatorial demeanour of the Prince de Condé, who, presuming on his services in the hour of peril, imagined that he might tyrannise over the Regent and her Minister.

He treated Mazarin and even Anne with ridicule, and under the influence of his intriguing sister, Madame de Longueville, formed a powerful faction among the disaffected nobles, and the party was distinguished by the name of the " young Fronde."

As the Duchesse de Chevreuse was very antagonistic to Condé, Mazarin thought fit what year to take her into his counsels.

One day in January, 1650, when the court as usual was assembled in the great gallery, the Cardinal drew Madame de Chevreuse into the embrasure of one of the windows, and said in his suavest manner, " I know you have many devoted friends, is it not possible to make them love us? If we could make use of some of them we might do great things. M. de Beaufort is at the service of Madame de Montbazon; she is devoted to Vigneul,—cannot we all work together, instead of against each other?" For one moment the fair *intrigante* thought she was about to be plunged into what she loved best, a political and secret intrigue; but happening to look up, she intercepted a glance between the Cardinal and the Queen, and she knew that the request for her assistance had been concerted between them.

"I quite understand your Eminence," she replied coldly, "and I will answer for both these men"; but Mazarin knew he had failed this time[1]—at least as far as her assistance could be relied on. With a bold stroke of authority he secretly effected an understanding with the Cardinal de Retz, the Duc de Beaufort, and other leaders of the original Fronde; and with their support, the Prince de Condé, the Prince de Conti, his brother, and the old Duc de Longueville, his brother-in-law, were all arrested and imprisoned at Vincennes.

The Cardinal next advised the Queen to go to Rouen, and work for the removal of the Duchesse de Longueville from Dieppe.

This journey was therefore carried out, and the King and Queen were received at Rouen with every mark of joy.[2] Anne sent at once an order to Dieppe for Madame de Longueville to join her old husband, who had been removed from Vincennes to Coulommiers, but this daring lady had no intention of giving up her position without a struggle. She feigned illness, and answered that

[1] *Mémoires de Retz.*
[2] *Mémoires de Montglat.*

she would obey the Queen's bequest when it was possible.

But this subterfuge did not avail her, and when she saw the royal troops under La Plessis-Bellière approach Dieppe she tried to win over the governor of that town to her side. She knew that could she succeed in holding Normandy, of which her husband had been governor, she would be rendering the greatest service to the royal princes.

She attempted to inflame the minds of the people against Mazarin, and told them how gloriously they would be serving their King if they would only open the gates to receive him, provided the hated Minister should be for ever excluded. The peace-loving inhabitants replied that they always did and always would serve their King, but they could not dictate to him who should be his adviser. At this answer Madame de Longueville was in despair, for failing support from within, and menaced by enemies without, she saw that her cause was lost.

She therefore determined on instant flight; she left the castle where she resided by a little postern door, which led outside the walls, followed by her women, and a few gentlemen of her suite who had courageously cast in their lot with hers.

Silently through the night she walked more than two miles to a small village on the coast, where they obtained a fishing-smack.

The weather was very boisterous, a gale having arisen, and the sailors were much against her starting, though all she requested of them was to put out to sea so as to get on board a large vessel in the offing.

But the wind being strong and the high tide coming in with such force that it was impossible to beach the little boat, she insisted on the men carrying her through the surf. As they were doing this a huge wave overwhelmed them, nearly sweeping them all out to sea, and they had the greatest difficulty in getting back with their burden to land.

As soon as Madame de Longueville had been brought round—for she had been rendered nearly unconscious—she wanted, in spite of the increasing tempest, to make the effort again; but this time none of the sailors would lend their aid, and she had to give up her intention.

Mounting a horse they procured, she rode pillion through the night to the house of a gentleman of her acquaintance who was willing to receive and befriend her. Being still bent on making her escape by water when the weather permitted, she sent a messenger to the ship, only to find out that the captain had been already bought by the Cardinal, and had she succeeded in getting on board she would have been arrested at once.

Nothing daunted, she sent to Havre and got the captain of a large trading-vessel to agree to give her a passage under a feigned name. She wished to pass as a nobleman who had fought a duel, and who was bound to make good his escape; by this means, and after many hardships, she eventually reached Flanders in safety.[1]

This intriguing woman had been a thorn in the flesh to the Queen and the Cardinal for many a day, and they hailed the news of her departure into exile with satisfaction. The enemies of Mazarin invariably met the same fate, their resistance was ineffectual when the all-powerful Minister was determined on their disgrace.

Though Madame de Longueville continued from afar to stir up rebellion, and sought to obtain an alliance with Spain inimical to the interests of France, all her machinations were of no avail as long as her enemy remained in office.

If hitherto Mazarin had triumphed, the net was closing round him also. It was said he could never turn his back without looking often behind him, and that his movements were impeded on every side.[2] The Duc d'Orleans now openly showed his hand. He came one evening early in 1651 to the Palais Royal, and with a courage he rarely displayed when dealing with the Cardinal, attacked him on all the points he had to find fault with. The Cardinal retorted that the *frondeurs* were real Cromwellians, and wanted to do in France what they had been doing in England. The Duke retorted that they were men of honour compared with the other party, and servants of the

---

[1] *Mémoires de Motteville.*

[2] Bazin la Raucon, *Histoire de France, sous le Ministère de Mazarin.*

King and the Crown. Mazarin attempting to argue, the Duc d'Orleans forced him to be silent, and, declaring that he had poisoned the young King's mind, refused even to remain in the same room with him.[1]

The following morning Mazarin, greatly incensed, handed over the charge of the King to the Maréchal de Villeroy.

The Duc d'Orleans now commanded the guards at the gates to take no orders but his own, and sent the coadjutor to announce to the *Parlement* that he declared himself in open opposition to the Minister.

This was the cause of a violent move on the part of the members. Some wanted to arrest the Cardinal, others to put him to death, and cries of " Long live the King! Down with Mazarin! " filled the air.

While this was going on, the Queen, on her side, was working to dissolve the Assembly unless they would listen to her wishes. She received the deputies, whom she had ordered to appear before her, in her bed, in the cap and night-clothes of a sick person. The Minister stood beside the royal couch with the Keeper of the Seals at his side.

The Queen spoke for a quarter of an hour with good sense and judgment. She regretted the loss of the Duc d'Orleans' friendship, but all her efforts were in vain. The following day

[1] This is confirmed by Tolon de Joly, Motteville, and others

the deputies again implored the Queen to give way and satisfy the wishes of her people, while the streets were filled with cries of "Let the Cardinal perish; send him away. We will not have Mazarin."

The Cardinal now thought it would be advisable to retire, at any rate for a short period, and he sought a private interview with Anne to tell her so.

She shed many tears, and tried to prevent his carrying out this project.

"I know we have failed, though you have tried to be master of everything in my name," she cried; "but our enemies are too many for us. But is it wise to leave altogether? And oh, what shall I do without you?"

With much tenderness Mazarin tried to cheer her.

"Queen of my heart," he said, "I do not willingly leave you, but I do think that at this crisis it is for the King's interest that I should resign. My absence need not be for ever, nor do I see what should prevent your following me, only let us be careful, and avoid giving rise to any suspicions as to my movements."

Sadly the Queen listened to his arguments, and agreed to his scheme. Perhaps she felt a soreness at his deserting her, and his proposal of a secret escape might have appeared a craven one. Mazarin was certainly not altogether free from cowardice, but the wily Italian by no means considered himself beaten, his retreat was part of the policy he had mapped out for himself. He had every intention of returning at a suitable moment, and Anne could follow out his orders and obey his instructions from his place of exile, just as well as she had ever done. His fertile brain was full of schemes for future aggrandisement and increased power. However, for the moment—but for the moment only—he had to admit that he was defeated, and he knew the value of the French proverb, " Reculer pour mieux sauter!"

CHAPTER XXII

MAZARIN IN EXILE

ON February 6, 1651, Mazarin attended the Queen's reception, and stood conversing with her for some time as was his wont. It was remarked that she looked pale, otherwise she appeared in her usual spirits, but the Queen and the Cardinal both knew that this casual conversation was in reality their last farewell. Anne was very calm, and gave no outward sign, although sorrow, anger, pity, and love must have mingled in her heart. She bade her Minister a careless good-night, and he left her side to join the throng of courtiers. His departure from the room made no stir; he sauntered out at the usual hour, talking and laughing on the way to his own apartments. All his preparations had been already made. He slipped on a red overcoat, took a plumed hat, and quietly left the Palais Royal by the side door in the Rue de Richelieu, accompanied by two gentlemen.[1] His horses and servants waiting for him were too common a spectacle to excite notice,

---

[1] Omer Talon said that two hundred horses were waiting for him in the Rue de Richelieu. De Brienne writes that this escort was waiting outside Paris for him.

and he rode quietly off to St. Germain through the darkness.

Anne covered his retreat by her calm impassiveness, but when Madame de Motteville next morning asked her how she was, her self-control at last gave way. Going to her oratory, and signing to this lady to follow her, she locked the door, and falling on her knees beside the altar she exclaimed:

"Judge for yourself as to the state I must be in. Is not the dismissal of my Minister evidence of my want of proper authority?"

Madame de Motteville, who, though not aware of his departure, believed it to be imminent, tried to console her mistress by pointing out that a change of ministry, and the appointment of a man who was in no way connected with the opposing factions, might tend to bring back her failing power.

"You are right," replied Anne sadly, "but God knows if I can find a disinterested man to serve me faithfully. I pray that the King at least may not suffer from any faults of the Cardinal, for I am well aware that he has faults; but he conducted affairs gloriously as long as he was left alone, and the first five years of my regency were very happy ones." She sank into a reverie after these words, and Madame de Motteville retired quietly, leaving her to seek consolation in prayer.

All through that day Anne bravely received visitors and transacted business as if nothing had happened, but when evening came she said to the one lady she had taken into her confidence,

"I wish it was always night—not that I can sleep, but at least I can have solitude and silence."

Poor lonely deserted Queen! Surely in the stillness of the great empty palace at St. Germain, Mazarin, occupied as was his mind with many schemes, was not so heartless as to forget the woman who had sacrificed so much for him.

When it was known in Paris that the Minister had left, the greatest excitement prevailed. In the *Parlement* they presented a vote of thanks to the Queen for having sent him away, but no one individual cared to commit himself on the subject. A wholesome fear of the great Cardinal still reigned; who could say whether he had really gone for good?

His departure seemed to have created a perfect panic; affairs were in chaos. When it was known that Anne designed to follow him, the leaders of the Fronde determined to frustrate this, and surrounded the palace with troops. It ended in the King and Queen-Regent being virtually prisoners in their own palace.

For a whole month Anne was unable to leave the Palais Royal. Every door was guarded, no one either on foot or in a carriage could go in or out without being searched, and every woman was unmasked to make certain she was not the Queen.

Anne tried to make light of the situation, and used to say laughingly her prison was charming, being her own house, but in her heart she felt the humiliation most keenly. When Mazarin heard to what straits his beloved mistress was subjected he determined to leave Havre, to which place he had gone in the hope of bringing it over altogether to his interests, and to proceed to Picardy, where he could cross the frontier, which might cause the wrath against him to subside.

He did not flee as an escaped criminal when once his exit from Paris was assured, but as a grand seigneur with a retinue of a hundred horses and men; he was unmolested most of the way, only at Abbeville they refused to let him pass through their town. From there he wrote a formal letter to the Queen, which was intended to be read publicly, sending in his resignation.

De Chauvigny was received at court as the future Minister, to the great disgust of Chateauneuf, who had expected to hold office himself; but the Queen had the greatest dislike to him, while De Chauvigny had always taken her part. She was, however, forced to write a document to be laid before the Senate, stating that the King and Queen-Regent, assisted by the Duc d'Orleans, the princes, the dukes, and peers of the kingdom, with the officers of the Crown, wished to state the resolution they had taken that Cardinal Mazarin should be for ever exiled from France.

Mazarin, when he found that it was useless for the present to think of returning, retired to Brühl, a little town in the electorate of Cologne, determined to take no part in the storm that was raging in the country of his adoption.

But though he nominally had retired from the government, he was carrying on a most animated correspondence with the Queen, and left but little to her guidance. Even Madame de Motteville, who would not admit any friendship—still less affection—between Anne and the Cardinal, had to admit that, though at a distance, his influence was as great as ever, and that when the dismissal of Chateauneuf from his office of Keeper of the Seals raised a perfect ferment " the Queen remained a long time without giving an answer because she was waiting for advice from Cardinal Mazarin." He still pulled the strings from behind the scenes, and not one move escaped him.

CHAPTER XXIII

THE CARDINAL'S CYPHER LETTERS

SOME letters written by Mazarin to the Queen at this period perhaps throw more light on their intimate relations than any other documents. They were originally written, more or less, in cypher; in 1836 they were collected and published with a key, which rendered them intelligible.[1]

Old letters, though interesting and curious, are not always entertaining, nor are these any exception to the rule. Readers, also, are apt to be incredulous, so much pretended historic information having been foisted on the public in this form: but the authenticity of these letters has been placed beyond dispute. As to their style, it is admitted that language was inflated at that period, expressions were used that conveyed much less than they appear to mean, and were more exaggerated than in the present day, and we must therefore make allowance for the time at which the Cardinal wrote. There is, however, little doubt that these letters to the Queen were

---

[1] These letters were edited with great care by M. Jules Ravernal, who was authorised by the "Conseil de la Société de l'Histoire de France" to undertake the work, and they were published at the society's expense. This appears to be a sufficient guarantee for their authenticity.

those of a lover, and are a lasting testimony of the deep attachment that existed between them.

No mention is made of this correspondence in the Memoirs of the day, for the reason that the letters had never been made known to the world, being jealously hidden away by the Queen, who alone must have possessed the key. It was not a very complicated one, though the meaning was purposely confused and rendered involved by the use of the masculine and feminine pronouns, quite irrespective of the sex of the person alluded to, and also by a variety of words and symbols being employed to express the same things and persons.[1] A portion of this key has been quoted below for the benefit of such readers as may take sufficient interest in cryptography to study these specimens of the Cardinal's letters.[2]

There were ninety-six in all, of which the greater number were written to Anne. Mazarin always Italianised his words, but the editor thought it better to reproduce the letters with ordinary French

---

[1] Sometimes the difference consisted in the size of the numerals, such as " 33," which stood for " Paris," and " ₃₃ " for " Bartet."

[2]
Amiens	The Queen	L'Ami .	Mazarin
Serafin .	,,	Sedan .	,,
42		Le Ciel	
22		48 .	
Zabaot .		44	
P	,,	200 .	,,
⸫ . .	,,	26 .	. ,,
La Fenetre	The Queen's affection	Confidant	The King
		La Barque	,,
Espagnol	The Queen's letters	D. .	,,
Ambition	Mazarin	22 .	,,
La Mer	,,	38 .	Le Sacre

orthography. The cypher was probably the Cardinal's own invention.

It is hardly credible that these letters, which were known to come from the Cardinal, should not have been intercepted by some one. Probably many more were despatched than ever reached their destination; indeed, all through the correspondence he writes constantly of the ever-present fear that the words he was inditing would not reach the person for whom they were intended. It was in one of these letters that he let fall an allusion which gave colour to the belief that he was actually married to the Queen. The pamphlets of the day spoke openly on the subject, and called it "un mariage de conscience."

Gabriel	Princesse Palatine	Le Sang .	Mme. de Chevreuse
45 .	,,	27 . . .	,,
46		L'Esprit .	,,
F . .	,,	42 . .	. Mme. de Beauvais
L'Ange	,,	Bruxelles	Mme. de Longueville
68 .	Duc de Mercœur	60	Le Président de Maison
69	,,	☉ . .	Le Président Viole
70	,,	61	. . . Siron
◇	,,	90	Les États-Généraux
La Confusion	Le Parlement	93	. Les Frondeurs
L'Ordre	,,	13 . .	. . . Condé
89 . .	,,	92 .	. . . . ,,
Silence . .	,,	34 .	Prince de Lyonne
Le Muet	Coadjutor de Gondé	Le Vieux	,,
41	,,	88 . . .	,,
La Vigne	- Bartet	11 . . .	. . Traité
64	,,	61 . . .	. . Siron
Dumont .		57 . . .	. de Chavigny
Le Président .	,,	⚡ Undying love of the Queen for the Cardinal
33 . . .	,,		
33	Paris		
20	Rome	*Equal devotion of the Cardinal for the Queen
103 .	Mme. de Chevreuse		

The Princesse Palatine, who was always rather inclined to scandal, wrote years afterwards, " The late Queen did worse than love Mazarin, she married him." But the very passion displayed in these letters rather points to the contrary. Had Mazarin been Anne's husband, he would have adopted a different tone, breathing affection more than passion. He adopts the language of romance, and reiterates his constant and unfailing devotion. He dreams of the happy moment when they will be reunited, and is ready to brave a thousand perils if he may but see her again. Anne, on her side, received these declarations with a love that remained unchanged. Pride, interest, and affection bound her fast; the voluminous correspondence was guarded by her as a sacred thing, and kept secret as far as it was possible. Here is one of the earliest of the collection.

LETTER 3

(Par Flein gentilhomme de M. de Mesme)

DE BRÜHL, *May* 11, 1651.

" My God, how happy and satisfied I should be if you could see my heart, or if I could write even one half of what I feel! If so, you could not fail to be of opinion that never has there existed a friendship approaching to that which I have for you. I will confess I never could have believed that it would have been so strong as to rob me of all happiness, and utterly to prevent my thinking of anything but you. But so it is, and I cannot do anything except what I think may be of service to you. I would wish also to express to you the hatred I feel for those mischief-makers who work without ceasing to cause you to forget me, and place obstacles in the way of our ever meeting again. In a word my hatred is in proportion to the love I bear you. But they are much mistaken if they expect to see in us any evil results from our prolonged absence from each other, and if l'Espagnol (*the Queen's letters*) were to say that the mountains of the Guadarrama had no right to place themselves between two such dear friends so . . . .[1]

"I quite believe all you write me of your affection, but I have a still better opinion of my own, for it reproaches me incessantly, because I do not give you sufficient proofs of its sincerity, and it also fills me with strange ideas, and makes me devise any number of wild and impracticable plans, which might bring me back to you. If I do not execute them it is because some are impossible, and others if worked out might cause you injury. But for that I would have thrown precaution to the winds, and hazarded my life over and over again if I might but see you once more. If our misfortunes do not find a speedy remedy I cannot answer for my prudence much longer, for such passion will overstep all bounds. Am I wrong in writing to you in this strain? If so I implore your pardon, but I think if I had been in your place I should

[1] Here followed five Spanish words which could not be deciphered.

have taken many steps to oblige l'Ami (*Mazarin*) to see me again.

"Yet, oh! how unjust I am, when I say that your love is not to be compared to mine! I beg a thousand pardons. You do more for me in one moment than I could do for you in a hundred years, and if you could realise how I am touched hy the words you write, you would in pity omit some of them, for they render me frantic when I dwell upon such a tender and constant affection while I am doomed to be absent from your side.

"All that you tell me about the Confidant (*the King*) charms me, and I really believe we shall receive satisfaction at last; but I tell you frankly that if the affairs of l'Ami (*Mazarin*) do not improve in the eyes of the State, I fear that all the good will of the Confidant (*the King*) will not be of much service. I assure you that all those who give you hope of his return, and tell you to wait in patience, are in reality working to prevent the possibility of such return, and mean to make the State responsible so as to have an excuse, and to be able to express their regret at the obstacle which will prevent the fulfilment of what they predicted. This is merely a passing reflection, but I beg of you to bear it in mind, for I know I am right. Since Adam, I think no one has been more worried than myself, though I am not one to complain; but I have been maltreated by those who were under the deepest obligations to me, so that it is impossible to keep silence—though I will willingly do so if the person that you wot of will continue to show me so much friendship with so much tenderness. It is for her that I speak, though there is enough to drive one mad when I think of France, and all the harm that may happen through this ingratitude.

"I am writing to you more openly than usual, because I know I can send you this letter with all safety; but I am reluctant to lay down my pen, for it is such happiness writing to you. However, I fear to tire you, so * * (*Mazarin's love*) adieu till to-morrow. Be ever ≋ (*the Queen's love*) for l'Ami (*Mazarin*) will be till death.*"

The following was one of the Cardinal's letters for the Queen's guidance, probably in response to one from herself asking for advice:—

Letter 31
July 18, 1651.

"I received, long after they were due, your two letters of the 5th and 8th inst. I cannot answer you as satisfactorily as I should wish, but I will tell you what I can in the time I have to spare, and the rest shall follow on another occasion, though the person who will speak to you on behalf of 26 (*Mazarin*) will explain the state of things, and what are the wishes of 46 (*Mazarin*). Remember what has occurred on the part of 57 (*Chavigny*) and 60 (*Président de Maisons*), and that it is the poor Ami (*Mazarin*) of Zabaot (*the Queen*) who is speaking to you, and that P (*the Queen*) has always promised *he* will refuse him nothing. Remember that 57 (*Chavigny*) is only working for the destruction of all that Zabaot (*the Queen*) loves best. I think therefore that Serafin (*the Queen*) should take great heed to the counsels of 46 (*Mazarin*) not only on account of the affection he bears towards *him*, but because in things both past and present 26 (*Mazarin*) is far more intelligent than those now in command. Do not trouble yourself by thinking that the action of 13 (*Condé*) has made things worse; but if you do not take some fixed resolve on which to act, everything will come to nought. A weak resolve will be better than none.

"It is absolutely necessary for my safety that I should change my place of residence. If the cry is raised that the Cardinal is approaching the frontier, be sure and say you have no knowledge of it.

"It would be advisable to show many things that I write you in these letters to 34 (*De Lyonne*) so that you can talk them over. It is necessary, too, that La Vigne (*Bartet*) should go over them also with Zabaot (*the Queen*), and consider them well. I do not know how I manage to live at all. I am alone, working without ceasing, and not in the most agreeable company; but so assured am I of the affection of Serafin (*the Queen*) that I count all else as less than nothing. It is a great solace to me reading the book sent me by 22 (*the Queen*), and I dream often of the second part of it. I must end this letter, but nothing can end the fact that I am yours, and believe me a thousand times always * (*Mazarin's love*)."

Letter 34

(Sent by La Cardonnerie, Lieut. of the Cardinal's guard)

July 27, 1651.

"As I am sending the bearer to inquire as to the healths of their Majesties, I take this opportunity to send you a word begging you to tell Zabaot (*the Queen*) that, notwithstanding that I wrote to 22 (*the Queen*), the Confidant (*the King*), Gabriel (*Princesse Palatine*), and others, and what I sent by other means to Serafin (*the Queen*), I think it right to represent to *him* by you, what 26 (*Mazarin*) has confided to me being of service to *him*. 44 (*Mazarin*) has learnt by experience what he may expect of 89 (*Le Parlement*), and the risk that he runs of losing the affection of 33 (*Paris*), and that Le Silence (*Parlement*) assisted by 92 (*Condé*) is fermenting discontent, and may oblige 21 (*the King*) to have 38 (*Le Sacre*) at 33 (*Paris*) to content 90 (*Les Etats-Généraux*), and that La Barque (*the King*) declaring his majority in Le Silence (*the Parlement*) may be constrained to receive 11 (*un traité*), and to ratify all declarations, so that the majority may set about the destruction of the Kingdom. King Charles did not receive such bad treatment from 73[1] as D (*the King*) and 44 (*Mazarin*), and yet his affairs were conducted at Rome. La Cardonnerie will tell you several things regarding the condition of 46 (*Princesse Palatine*), or will let you know through 64 (*Bartet*). Above all things I implore you to say from me to ♉ (*the Queen*) that *he* is not to be anxious, and if good health be granted all will yet go well. I beg you to embrace Confidant (*the King*) for me, and tell him a thousand things about the affection I bear towards him. I will say nothing further save * (*Mazarin's love*)."

Letter 43

August 22, 1651.

"I have not even the consolation of writing to you with the liberty I should wish. It is no small comfort to open one's heart to a true friend in time of affliction, and, from what I learn, they are diligently trying to intercept our letters, so it would be an act of great imprudence to hazard anything of a private nature; it is a time of suffering for us both, and we must put up with it. If it had only pleased God that I alone should bear this pain, and that 22 (*the Queen*) could have been spared, I should be thankful. This last post has brought me no letters from P (*the Queen*) nor from 42 (*Madame de Beauvais*), nor from hardly any one. I thought at least Gabriel (*Princesse Palatine*) would have written me a line. Please God, all has passed off

[1] This number has not been decyphered.

well. Le Brun alone sends me word that he saw plainly that Serafin (*the Queen*) had taken a resolution, and I hope more than ever that *he* has given up the friendship with 57 (*Chavigny*). I implore you ever to say ⁂ (*Queen's devotion*) in return for * (*Mazarin's love*), which is the same thing I wrote you last time, for it is absolutely true."

LETTER 53
September 26, 1651.

"Ten times I have taken my pen in my hand without having been able to write to you, and I am so beside myself with the blow that I have received, that I do not know whether the words I write, have any rhyme or reason. The King and Queen, by an authentic act, have declared me to be a traitor. I have no longer any peace of mind.[1] I am sure that when the Queen learns the deplorable state to which I am reduced she will be filled with regret, but that will not prevent all Europe learning, in fifteen days, that Cardinal Mazarin is the most abominable of men! I swear to you, that in the state I am in I am ashamed to face even my servants. I no longer sleep; in fact, you would hardly recognise me. It is in the Queen's power to prevent this news spreading if she will take prompt action, and I count it among my misfortunes that I am obliged to importune her, but what else

---

[1] Declaration of the King and Queen Regent to the Parlement on the subject of the perpetual exile of Cardinal Mazarin, August 17, 1651.

can I do? to whom else can I lay bare my trouble? I see she answers for 61 (*Siron*), and says that he and 35 (*Madame d'Aigullon*) are my most dangerous enemies, and that they are working in concert with 57 (*Chavigny*), and with access to ☉ (*President Viole*), and that there are great cabals at court. Also that it has been suggested that 26 (*Mazarin*) should make a journey to Rome. However, I still give you my word that nothing can alter my love towards P (*the Queen*) even if *he* signed my death-warrant. And I am persuaded *he* has the same sentiment towards me, and I am ever *his* devoted servant, with the same passion as of old. To my last breath I am * *, and a million times *, and my greatest joy is to know that these sentiments do not displease you, and that you are ever ⚎."

The following letter has been often quoted in support of the theory of the secret marriage :—

LETTER 63

October 22, 1651.

" I am persuaded that the hearts of the Queen and myself are united by ties that cannot be broken either by time or by the efforts of men. I have seen a letter from the Queen in which she said that her last thought would be for me. You cannot think how such a sentiment remains for ever in my heart. God must have inspired these words, for at that time I was in a state of extreme prostration, and needed some help. It is strange to find myself both married and separated, and always pursued by obstacles to this marriage. I at least hope that nothing will prevent my seeing her who is dearer than life itself."

Once more there comes a letter of counsel when Anne, distraught by the state of affairs, appealed to her chief adviser for help.

LETTER 74

November 17, 1651.

"You will readily believe the joy of Le Ciel (*Mazarin*) when La Cardonnerie arrived with beautiful presents for him, from both 21 (*the King*) and P (*the Queen*). I cannot write at length to-day, but I shall try and send you a line every morning. I think I may venture to say that Le Ciel (*Mazarin*) will get you out of your difficulties if you give him time, and above all if you do not precipitate matters. I forgot to tell you that 93 (*les frondeurs*) are of the same opinion as l'Ami (*Mazarin*) and Gabriel (*Princesse Palatine*), and this is most important. Believe that 44 (*Mazarin*) has real knowledge of the state of affairs, and that you will assuredly come out well if you confide in these two persons only. I beg of you to tell Confidant (*the King*) that Là Mer (*Mazarin*) will not see him without his parent, and that he and she would die a thousand deaths for him, and above all for her who is dearest to him, as she is to * who believes in ≋."

The last of the series was dated January 17, 1652, the year that witnessed the Cardinal's triumphant return to France.

Letter 96

January 17, 1652.

"I received your letter of the 8th with the greatest pleasure, as you can well believe, for nothing in this world equals for me the knowledge that I am more and more assured of the great honour of your constant friendship. I am waiting with infinite impatience to know what will occur at the interview between La Mer (*Mazarin*) and 22 (*the Queen*), but I think 22 will be satisfied with La Mer, because 26 (*Mazarin*), who is his greatest friend, assured me of this.

"I have been told Le Ciel (*Mazarin*) greatly desires to see Zabaot (*the Queen*) in private, but I fear it will be difficult to manage. As to the Cardinal, who was threatened that if he ever appeared in France again he would be torn to pieces by the populace, he is very well, and has been loaded with civilities wherever he has been. He was in despair, however, that the excellent M. de Beaufort had not been able to carry out his resolution. After the exploit of this latter in Paris, when he arrested the Comtesse d'Harcourt, he announced that he intended to arrive with their

Royal Highnesses' Cavalry, and cut in pieces all the *Mazarins*. He did not, however, succeed in getting there as soon as the Marquis de Sourdis, so the glorious action which would have carried down his name to posterity miscarried altogether. The bearer of this letter will inform you of many things I have not written, and I will not keep him longer, as it would retard the departure of Fleins. I am told a party of assassins have gone to Paris with the express intention of murdering the Cardinal, and they received the blessing of M. de Beaufort before they started. I can assure you, however, that this causes him no uneasiness, and the bearer will tell you how calmly he sets out on his journeys, fearing nothing. But my messenger cannot tell you how much I am * (*Mazarin's devotion*). You may be able to some extent to guess because 26 (*Mazarin*) knows what is the meaning of ⚌ (*Queen's devotion*), and he hopes to explain it to the satisfaction of Zabaot (*the Queen*) as soon as he sees P (*the Queen*)."[1]

The time had now come when the Cardinal considered he could safely return to court, and the need for correspondence was at an end. It must have occupied much of his leisure, and the search for trusty messengers to convey these tokens of his undying affection must have given him in-

[1] Their meeting took place on January 28, ten days after the above letter was written, at Poitiers, where Mazarin made his entrance into France in company with the King, who, hearing of his near approach, went out to meet him.

finite trouble, and been a work of no small difficulty. It has been affirmed that Mazarin's ardour greatly cooled after his return, and that he found it ridiculous or at any rate inconvenient to keep up this appearance of romantic love; but the further story of his own life and that of the Queen hardly confirms this, though doubtless growing years and infirmities rendered his temper uncertain and his companionship less ideal than it had been. But Anne's love was strong enough to overcome all such obstacles. These letters existed as a proof of what they were to each other; she treasured them as her greatest consolation and solace through the weary months of their separation, and they remained hidden during the rest of her life, a most sacred possession. Woman-like, she was willing to make every allowance for the man she loved, so that whether Mazarin was far or near, the union of their hearts remained unbroken.

CHAPTER XXIV

THE RETURN OF MAZARIN

IN Paris during this period social life continued, both in the capital and in the palace, much as before. Discontent was rife abroad, and intrigues abounded in the court circle. A marriage had been arranged between the Prince de Conti and Mademoiselle de Chevreuse, she and her mother having once more returned to Paris. Madame de Longueville, who had also been allowed to come back to Paris, was entirely opposed to this match. She had no desire to have as a sister-in-law a young and pretty woman who would eclipse her in society, and she worked on her brother in such a manner as to make him abandon the idea. The Queen, who dreaded the marriage, which she thought might prove prejudicial to her interests, saw with pleasure the obstacles that Madame de Longueville put in the way of it, and the service this lady was thus rendering caused Anne to receive her with more kindness than had at first been her intention.

The Prince de Conti was indifferent to Mademoiselle de Chevreuse, though he had no active dislike to her; but he was quite ready to fall in with his clever sister's views, and soon disgusted the young lady by his want of devotion. Moreover he made no excuses to the Duchesse de Chevreuse, but coolly told her he would withdraw.

Naturally her anger at this treatment was very great. She had always sided with his party, and now she determined to be entirely on the other side. She at once went to the Queen with offers of assistance in any way that she could be of use to her, and by her actions at this time greatly contributed to the return of Mazarin.

Madame de Longueville on her part had no desire to quarrel with the Queen, and sent her word that she was entirely at her service. She sent her friend the Princesse Palatine to interview Anne, and this Princess also despatched M. Bartet to the Cardinal to assure him of Madame de Longueville's affection.

So did these intriguing women work in this underhand manner while professing the utmost devotion to the Crown.

Many people were in communication with the Cardinal, for the general opinion was that he would return. For one thing it was well known that the Queen gave no answer to questions of State importance till she had had time to consult the Cardinal.

Mazarin was living still at Brühl with his nieces, in great comfort, surrounded by his friends, when a rumour went abroad that the Duc de Mercœur had married Mademoiselle Mancini without asking the consent of the King, having joined the Cardinal's family at Brühl, where the ceremony was openly performed. De Mercœur then returned to Paris, where he was interrogated by the *Parlement* as to the truth of the story.

He first said he did not consider that he was bound to reply to their question, but he assured the assembly that had he done so it would have been no crime.

"You mean to say," said the First President, "that you married her before her uncle was pronounced to be a criminal."

De Mercœur answered, Yes. He had married her before the Cardinal had gone into exile.

This was obviously untrue. The Duc de Mercœur had married Mademoiselle Mancini during his visit to Brühl, and had openly declared that his Eminence was not wanting in friends ready to draw their swords on his behalf if his return to Paris was opposed.

Thus the idea that Mazarin would return began gradually to permeate all classes.

On September 17 it was arranged that King Louis XIV. should make a public entry into the Halls of Justice to declare his majority. He was only thirteen years of age, but in those days of precocious men and women he was considered fit to reign as King, and had reached the age when his future marriage could already be discussed.

The pleasure-loving Parisians flocked to this fête as gaily as if never a cloud had darkened their city, and gazed their fill on the goodly procession and the handsome young King in their midst. All the princes of the blood, and the dukes and duchesses of France, laid aside their quarrels and gathered together to do honour to the occasion.

The Queen, accompanied by Monsieur, the King's little brother and heir-presumptive to the throne, repaired in state to greet him. A splendid company of light horsemen, with glittering coats of gold-and-silver cloth, preceded by the band, led the way, and the cavalry lined the road to keep back the excited populace, whose cries of "Vive le Roi!" rent the air.

Louis wore a coat so completely covered with gold embroidery that the colour of it was not visible. He was tall for his age, and looked more than his thirteen years. He was decorated with orders, and sparkling with jewels, and looked already every inch the "*Grand Monarque*" that he continued to be all his life.

Anne, in her royal robes, a beautiful woman in spite of her fifty years, with her face wreathed in smiles, seemed by no means sad to see her Regency at an end, and to be able to lay down the burden of government: if she had a sorrow, it was that she could not place her son at this critical moment in the hands of the man she considered so well calculated to guide him.

She loved her King tenderly, and without a tinge of jealousy could truly say, "May he be master and I be nought."

Her desire was to return in peace to Val-de-

Grace, but Louis was far too young, and the country too disturbed for such an idea to be entertained for a moment.

Indeed, Anne found that a good deal of work still fell to her share. Chateauneuf was Minister just then. The Prince de Condé hated him so intensely, and was so opposed to his measures, that there were moments when he would not have been averse from seeing his old enemy Mazarin back in power.

It is needless to say Anne longed for his return, not only from her personal feelings, but, apart from that, she saw how necessary his powerful government was to put the King in his proper place, and not to let the people of France think that the Monarch was a mere puppet in their hands, and to be made to do their good pleasure.

She considered that Chateauneuf served them well on the whole, while his friends, not wishing him to be deposed by Condé, gave out everywhere that the King's affairs were prospering, that Condé was more than half defeated, and if Mazarin did return, it would only be a pretext to prolong the war now raging in the west of France between the King's troops and those of the insurgents.

One day, when the Duchesse de Navailles was seated in conversation with the Queen, she told her how many persons were in favour of the Cardinal's return.

"I am aware of this," replied Anne, "and both his Majesty and myself greatly need a Minister who is absolutely one with us, and by whom we could control the incessant intrigues at court. I know that the insolence of the Chamber of Deputies deserves to be punished, but at the same time I fear that if the Cardinal returns too soon it may be a danger to himself, which would but add to our difficulties, therefore I dare not yet take steps in the matter."[1]

The Duchess and her husband were devoted friends of Mazarin, and instead of seeing in these words a mark of the Queen's wisdom and prudence, she thought it augured ill for him, and that the Queen's sentiments towards him were changed. She therefore made her husband write promptly to the Cardinal, telling him his cause was lost unless he returned at once.

The effect of this letter was to make Mazarin put his affairs in order without loss of time, not without anger in his heart at Anne failing, perhaps from cowardice, to support his interests. This did not, however, prevent his continuing his correspondence in the same strain, and he sent her his diary, with instructions to keep it with the greatest care.

Fifteen months had passed since Mazarin had fled in secret from Paris, and he was fully determined to return.

His nieces had been living with him, and but for his disgrace and absence from court he had been leading a very pleasant existence, surrounded by all the luxury so dear to him. When

[1] *Mémoires de Motteville*, vol. 3.

there was a talk of his departure his house steward had some trouble in winding up his affairs, and checking the reckless extravagance

And now another woman meddled in the affairs of the Cardinal, as she too was desirous to have the honour of settling what was the most momentous crisis in Europe.

This was Madame de Châtillon, a beautiful widow, who cherished a bitter hatred for Madame de Longueville.

This lady had many a score to pay off on Madame de Longueville, who had robbed her of her admirers more than once; she was, besides, in love with the Duc de Nemours, and, being anxious to win his approbation as well as to enrich herself, she thought if she could aid in peace being made, without her rival having anything to say to it, she would greatly advance her plans. She went to the Duc de Nemours and laid her scheme before him, begging him to procure for her full powers to treat with the Cardinal.

Mazarin was doubtful whether this wily woman, in spite of her rank and her charms, was equal to such a task—rather he thought that she was a tool in the hands of the Princes; but with his usual caution he played a waiting game.

He was more crafty and far more clever than his opponents, and saw a means of deriving solid benefit from the negotiations which were being worked on his behalf.

Turenne had obtained a victory over Condé in a

sortie at Étampes, on June 19th, 1652, and this made Mazarin more than ever determined to march to his relief with the royal troops. He had hoped to get Charles IV., Duc de Lorraine, brother of the Duchesse d'Orleans, to aid him, but he found he was outbid by the princes, who had bribed him to take their part.

The battle now raged at their gates, and it was a struggle between Condé and Turenne as to who should be master of the capital. Many valuable lives were lost in the combat at the Porte Saint Antoine, on July 2nd, 1652, among others young Mancini, a brave and valiant youth, who paid with his life for the misfortunes of his uncle, who was indeed accredited with being the cause of all the trouble.

Mazarin now resolved to return to Paris without delay. He greatly disliked the idea of the long march, and was often filled with alarms, and wished he had never undertaken it; but making a virtue of necessity he set off on his dangerous undertaking, fully expecting that the Duc d'Orleans would oppose his passage through the country, and especially at the rivers, where it would have been easy to turn him back.

With his followers and his handful of troops he, however, overcame all difficulties, and his near arrival was soon heralded. Having gone to the relief of Turenne, on his way, they together besieged Bar-le-Duc, and the reinforcements of Mazarin turned the tide of victory. There was nothing now to prevent his triumphant return.

M. de Tellier was first sent out to meet and escort the Cardinal, and then Louis determined to go himself to receive the exiled, but now victorious, Mazarin. The meeting was at Pontoise, whither Anne had already gone, on February 9, 1653. Crowds had assembled to witness the arrival—the favourite of the moment never lacked friends and admirers; M. de Chateauneuf and the Comte de Brienne were in waiting at the time, and in attendance in the Queen's room.

They discreetly retired, however, feeling sure that the formal salutations between their Majesties and the *ci-devant* Minister would give place to a somewhat more tender greeting.

And so it was. Mazarin's first words, as he held Anne's hand to his lips, were to thank her and her son for all their love and kindness toward him, and then, as he saw the rising emotion of the Queen, he turned the conversation to a lighter vein, and began entertaining them with an account of his adventures. The next day the Cardinal received all those who desired to pay him their respects. He was proud of the reception that had been given him; but while loading with caresses those who had proved themselves his friends, he hardly tried to conceal his coldness and indifference towards those whom he had good reason to suspect of enmity. The Comte de Brienne was among this number, in his memoirs he records the fact in these words,

"I had never been among those who paid

assiduous court to the Cardinal—indeed, we had had many an encounter of sharp words.

"I was in attendance on her Majesty when Mazarin returned, and, not caring to see him, I sought to be in her presence at an hour when I thought it least likely to meet the Cardinal. The Queen soon perceived this—indeed, Mazarin complained to her of my want of courtesy—and she begged me as a personal favour to go and pay my respects to him.

"This I of course at once did. I saw little change in him, save that his absence had made him, if possible, prouder and more haughty than ever."[1]

His return to Paris was one long triumph, and once more France was under his powerful dominion. The people who had tried to persuade themselves they despised him, feared him still, as they had done before, and argued that his rule was better than the imaginary liberty they had hoped to enjoy without him, but which had never come to pass.

From passive endurance they soon began to exalt him, and offer incense at his shrine, and his faults were forgotten by the fickle people, who now saw nothing but wisdom in his actions.

The magistrates came to offer him their homage— he had the air of a sovereign taking possession of his state—and the princes and the principal nobles aspired to his favour. His first act was to

[1] *Mémoires de Brienne.*

put a speedy end to the civil war at Bordeaux; he at once put the army on a better footing, wishing to make them ready to defend their country from foreign foes, instead of merely waging war on their fellow-countrymen. France felt once more that the Cardinal was at the head of affairs, and master of her destinies.

CHAPTER XXV

MAZARIN AGAIN IN POWER

IT was the general belief that the Queen awaited the Cardinal's return with eagerness, and received him with transports of joy; others say she had learnt to do without him, and received him coldly.

As a French historian puts it, "there are mysteries of a woman's heart which a man cannot penetrate, and he would be bold who would try to understand them."[1]

Anne's real chronicler, Madame de Motteville, maintains a complete silence on the subject in her voluminous *Mémoires*, in which she mentions the Cardinal as little as· possible, save in his public capacity.

But in those days the world had not been privileged to see the letters still hidden under lock and key in the Queen's private coffer—letters which tell their own tale, and refute emphatically the statement of Anne's coldness or indifference.

The years now rolled by in peace and tranquillity as far as Anne and her court were concerned.

---

[1] Bazin de Rancon, *Histoire de France sous le Ministère de Mazarin*, vol. 2, p. 207.

Mazarin, whose palace had been despoiled in his absence, began to collect fresh treasures.

"Ce grand spoliateur," as he was termed, was supposed to be reduced to poverty. On returning to his palace he found nothing but bare walls, but he at once began to buy back, piece by piece, all that he had lost. Nearly everything was brought back to him, even precious manuscripts, which this time he had the wisdom to have entered into a catalogue, which is mentioned in the *Historical Researches of Antiquities in Paris.*

His books having been dispersed, the King's library was brought to form the nucleus for a new one. Jabach, a German banker, and amateur collector, had bought most of the pictures, and Mazarin managed to get them back by degrees, and the famous Palais Mazarin soon became more of a world-wonder than ever. He instituted a famous lottery of 500,000 livres' worth of curios and jewels, and gave a number of tickets gratis to the King and all the members of the royal family; but there was a method in all these proceedings which was easy to follow—he was lavish in his generosity if he thought it to his advantage. It was the fashion to accuse him of avarice, but "extravagance" seems a more fitting word to use, at any rate where his own expenditure was concerned.

Meanwhile, the estimation in which he was held increased daily, and one and all paid court assidu-

[1] *Sauval*, vol. ii.

ously to the great man; his nieces were also a source of admiration and interest.

The marriage of Madame de Mercœur had elevated them all into a fine position. Her sister Olympe, though less pretty, was equally attractive. Her features were far from perfect, but the thin, sallow girl she had been when young and unformed had grown into a pretty woman. Her eyes were full of fire, and her complexion clear, she was on a rather large scale, but had small hands. With all her charms, she was still unmarried.[1] The King adored her, but of course at his tender age it was only a matter of amusement to Anne.

Olympe was very discreet, knowing full well she could not aspire to be Queen. Various matches had been proposed for her, one with the son of the Maréchal de la Meilleraye, but she had refused him. She wanted to be a princess. Her cousin, Mademoiselle de Martinozzi, having become engaged to the Prince de Conti, she had no idea of being eclipsed by her, and indeed, she did not hide her annoyance the day that the marriage was celebrated. Besides, what added to the sting was the fact that the Prince had been given the choice of the two girls, and had far preferred the gentle Martinozzi.[2]

Mazarin had hitherto stood aloof in matters connected with his nieces, but the growing infatuation of the King called for some attention.[3]

---

[1] Amédée René, *Nièces de Mazarin.*
[2] *Mémoires de Motteville.*
[3] Other authorities affirm that Mademoiselle de Martinozzi married Prince Alphonse d'Este.—*Mémoires de l'Abbé de Choisy.*

The Cardinal doubtless knew that he could safely leave his niece to bring this episode to a close, nevertheless he thought it advisable to silence the tongues of the scandal-mongers by taking a high stand. Olympe, who was older than the King, knew well that though for the moment the boy fancied himself in love, it was really only a youthful passing fancy. She did not play willingly into her uncle's hands, for she considered that he had been very neglectful of her interests all this time in not having furthered any suitable alliance for her. She saw rather that he had made a tool of her, being well aware that while she remained at court she amused the King, and warded off other and more dangerous beauties.

Left to herself, and seeing that Anne took little real interest in her, Olympe determined to satisfy her ambitions, and she agreed to marry Eugéne, Comte de Soissons, son of one of the Princes of Savoy. He was a great-grandson of Charles V., through his grandmother, and of royal French blood through his mother the Princesse de Carignan, so it would have been difficult indeed for Olympe to make a better marriage than this, and, moreover, the prince was a man whom in every way she could respect and love.

When it came to the point the King, in spite of his wail of undying love, appeared quite indifferent when witnessing the marriage ceremony, and Anne, who was vexed at the very idea that her son should have fretted after Mademoiselle Mancini, turned to the Cardinal, and said triumphantly, "Did I not tell you there was nothing to fear in this attachment?"[1]

The Cardinal about this time was much taken up by family claims. Both his sisters, Madame de Martinozzi and Madame Mancini, being widows, had come to live in Paris, where, being charming and intelligent women, they were much appreciated, and when Madame Mancini died it was a real grief to many, as well as to Mazarin, who was tenderly attached to her.

It was all the more sad as Madame de Mercœur died in her confinement a few days after her mother, leaving three little boys. The whole family was therefore plunged in a double mourning. When on her deathbed, Madame Mancini commended her younger children, a boy and three more girls, to the care of her brother, especially imploring him to put the third daughter, Marie, into a convent, instead of letting her appear at court, because she considered that the girl's character and temperament would lead her into temptation. The remaining two, Hortense and Marianne, were still little more than children.

Mazarin, however, disregarded this request. He sent to Italy for the youngest, Marianne, who had been left there at school by her mother, and removed the others from the convent near Paris where they were being educated.

Whether the Cardinal disapproved of convents,

[1] *Mémoires de Motteville.*

or whether it was natural affection which made him wish to keep them all with him—for he really loved these young girls—cannot now be decided; at any rate he took them to live with him.

Hortense already gave promise of being the most beautiful of them all. Marie, the eldest of these three, was thin and sallow, as Olympe had been, and was ungainly in appearance. She inherited much of her uncle's nature, and was proud and arrogant. Nevertheless, the impressionable Louis now transferred his admiration to her, and she took full advantage of the young King's innocent attentions, for she found it greatly improved her position at court. He sought her out on every occasion, led her out to dance, and paid her a thousand little attentions. She became the envy of all the other ladies, and it caused a great deal of jealousy and heart-burning, but, under the protection of her uncle, Marie enjoyed her triumph unmolested.

One evening Anne had begged Henrietta Maria to come to a small and friendly entertainment in her private room to see the King dance. She was asked to bring her little daughter, only ladies of the court and young girls being admitted.

The Queen appeared in a cap and *négligé* dress—some equivalent to the modern tea-gown—to mark the informality of the occasion; but though the company was small, much care had been lavished on the arrangements, so that the party should be in accordance with the exalted rank of those present. The King, always accustomed to pay every attention to the Cardinal's nieces, at once led out Marie Mancini to dance the *branle*, a sort of country dance of which he was very fond.

His mother, much annoyed at such lack of manners, rose hastily from her chair, and taking his partner by the arm pulled her away, and ordered them to desist, telling Louis in an angry whisper to lead out his cousin, the Princess of England.

Henrietta Maria, who saw what was going on, and did not want the young people's evening to be spoilt, ran up to her sister-in-law, and begged her not to mind whom the King danced with, all the more as her child had hurt her foot, and was, she thought, incapable of dancing.

"No," replied the Queen, " I cannot allow such an excuse. If Louis cannot dance with his cousin, he shall not dance with any one else; but I know he will wish to do so—it was only forgetfulness on his part. Come here, Louis, and lead out Mademoiselle d'Angleterre."

But Louis was not going to be dictated to, and in spite of his mother's remonstrances and entreaties he turned sulky, and answered rudely that he would not dance with little girls.

It was true his cousin was only eleven, but he was only sixteen, and Anne was very angry indeed.

In public she always treated the King with great respect, but in private she allowed herself the privilege of a mother to scold him heartily.

Both the Queen and the Cardinal now saw that

it would be very difficult to guide Louis aright, for he fell in love over and over again, the only safety being in his fickle nature. He hardly ever saw the Comtesse de Soissons now, and appeared quite indifferent to her.

To Hortense he paid but scant attention, in spite of her beauty. He did not find little girls to his taste.

It was said that the King was in much better temper ever since his adoration for Marie, that she had a good influence over him, and used to advise him to read novels, and amuse himself in many ways.[1] It was now thought best to arrange a marriage for the King, and as there was some prospect of peace with Spain, Mazarin's thoughts turned in that direction. Affairs of State were so intricate at that epoch that the Cardinal found his hands pretty full, and to the Envoy Louis de Haro Mazarin made the famous speech:

"You Spanish Ministers are fortunate, and can discuss matters with ease. Your women are amenable to government, their only passions are luxury and vanity, and they are occupied with writing letters to their lovers and confessors. But in France it is quite different, they mix themselves up in the affairs of State. We have three such, the Duchesse de Longueville, the Duchesse de Chevreuse, and the Princesse Palatine, who alone are enough to upset any country."[2]

[1] *Mémoires de Mademoiselle, Coll. Petitot.*
[2] *Vie de Madame de Longueville, par Villefois,* 2nd part.

Now he had to add to his list the young girls who fluttered round the Monarch.

A Spanish alliance, if it could be brought about, appeared to be far the most politic. Anne would have welcomed the little English princess as her daughter-in-law, but the King continued to feel aversion to his little cousin, which sentiment was fostered by the Cardinal, who disapproved of the match.

CHAPTER XXVI

A WIFE FOR LOUIS XIV

A QUESTION now arose as to whether it would not be a good plan for the King to marry Princesse Marguerite of Savoy. Mazarin was of opinion that the match that would really suit the Queen best, and serve his own ends, was the Spanish one, so, after his Machiavellian habit, he encouraged the King to pay court to Princesse Marguerite, taking care that the news should reach the ears of the King of Spain, and, by making him think that the prize was slipping out of his grasp, render him more desirous to see his own daughter on the throne of France.

On the other hand, if the Spanish King would not lend himself to the project, they could but fall back on the House of Savoy.

As long as the King did not marry the daughter of Henrietta Maria, Mazarin was content, whichever way things went—and, after all, the Princess of Savoy was first cousin by marriage to his own niece, the Comtesse de Soissons, which was not unpleasing to his vanity. So, in accordance with his policy, he arranged that the court should proceed to Lyons in the end of November, 1658, to meet the royal family of Savoy, and Anne, ever pliable in his hands, agreed to everything he proposed.

The King was full of impatience to see his promised bride, and when he heard that the Cardinal intended to go out to meet them, he declared he must do so as well.

Accompanied by Monsieur his brother and his mother, they started in the royal coaches, and drove a few miles out of Lyons, where the court was staying. Anne remained at the place appointed for the meeting, but the King got out, and, mounting his horse, rode on in advance to meet the Princess of Savoy and her daughters.

After the usual salutations, during which his eyes were fixed intently on the Princesse Marguerite, he returned to his mother's carriage, and exclaimed,

"She is charming, very much like her picture. She is rather swarthy, certainly, but has a pretty figure."

The Queen then alighted from her coach and went forward to embrace the royal strangers. She politely offered a seat in her carriage to the Princess; Monsieur escorted the elder sister, who was a young widow, and the King handed Princesse Marguerite into the state coach, where he made himself very pleasant to her all the way back to Lyons.

There they were all received with great state, and the Princess publicly thanked both the King and the Cardinal for the kindness and honours with which they had been welcomed.[1]

[1] *Mémoires de Motteville*, vol. 4.

The evening passed off well, but destiny and the Cardinal intended quite another marriage for Louis XIV., and this poor young princess had merely been made to play a part, without any regard for her own feelings or natural ambitions.

When the King of Spain saw that the French alliance was slipping away from his grasp, he became, as the Cardinal had anticipated, more keen to ratify it.

"It cannot be, it shall not be," was the Monarch's answer when told that the royal family of Savoy were shortly expected in France, with a view to the settlement of the marriage. He sent for Don Antonio Pimental, to whom he confided the delicate mission of conferring with the Cardinal, and offering him peace and the Infanta. In such haste was he that he sent off Pimental without passports at the risk of being taken prisoner. The latter, however, had no fears; whether a prisoner or not he had every intention of treating directly with the Minister, and he knew that what he had to propose would ensure a favourable hearing.

Wearing a disguise, he made his way safely to Lyons, arriving on the very day on which the Princesses of Savoy made their State entrance. Don Antonio Pimental came into the city from the opposite side, and thus these two powers were to be pitted against each other in the arena, and Louis XIV. was to be the prize.

The combat was unfair from the beginning. The little principality of Savoy was no match for the great kingdom of Spain, backed up, as the latter was, by the all-powerful Mazarin.

Pimental did not avow his intention too openly, but sent for a man named Colbert, the Cardinal's steward, and discovering his identity to him begged for a private interview with the Minister.[1]

While this intrigue was going on. Anne on her side was in a state of great depression. She was much disappointed in the Princesse Marguerite, who was not nearly so pretty as she expected, and in her heart she had always hankered after the marriage of her son with one of his own family.

It is hardly to be supposed that she was not privy to the Cardinal's intentions, though it is possible that he did not always confide his plans to her. She did not find it altogether easy to persuade Louis to give up the princess to whom he had taken a fancy, and he told his mother he would marry her, and that her arguments were of no avail, for he was now master of his actions.

Anne burst into tears—the poor woman invariably found herself between two fires. How was she to content both her son and her lover?

As usual she had recourse to her prayers, and sent for her confessor, begging him to have petitions offered up in all the convents on her behalf.[2]

That evening when the court were assembled the Comte de Beringhen, who had been watching

[1] Colbert, who at that time merely held the post of steward in the Cardinal's household, rose to eminence, and became the great Minister of Louis XIV.

[2] *Mémoires de Motteville*, vol. 4.

the King's lover-like attentions towards Princesse Marguerite, and saw that the Queen regarded them with an anxious air, approached her, and said:

"What do you say to all this, Madame, and what does the Cardinal say?"

"He does not say much as yet," was Anne's cautious reply, "and I hardly know what steps to take to check the King's impetuosity."

Beringhen, who was devoted to the Queen, to whom he owed all his advancement, went off after this conversation to seek the Cardinal, and pointed out to him the obligation he was under to oppose the inclinations of the Monarch, and fall in with the views of the Queen in this matter.

"I do not see," replied Mazarin calmly, "what concern it is of mine. It is not my fault if the King is too much devoted to this young lady, and I certainly have no intention of mixing myself up in his affairs."

Though the Cardinal replied with due courtesy to the rather tactless remonstrances of the well-meaning but impetuous Beringhen, the answer the latter received left him no doubt, that his remarks were useless and unavailing.

It was Mazarin's custom always to give a polite and evasive reply. When people worried him with questions of the kind, or proffered him advice, the discomfited ones always retired with the certainty that he was laughing in his sleeves all the time, and never would he admit for one instant in public that the Queen was swayed by him.

The following evening Mazarin entered Anne's private room with a smiling face.

She was seated alone, looking very disconsolate, but brightened up at the sight of the Cardinal's cheerful countenance.

"Good news, Madame," he exclaimed.

"What news can be good save that of peace with Spain?" replied the lady.

"I bring you better news even than that. I come to announce to your Majesty peace, *and* the Infanta!"

Anne sprang from her chair with sparkling eyes, all her lassitude gone, and clasped Mazarin's hand in both of her own. This was indeed the desire of her heart, about to be fulfilled.

After a short and eager conversation they sent for Louis. Even that fickle youth, who only wanted to be married, and did not much care who the lady was, had sense enough to cast his mind into futurity, and see what such a union would mean for himself and for his country, and without an instant's hesitation he agreed to everything. There was considerable awkwardness as to how the news was to be broken to the Princess of Savoy, but the Cardinal was equal to the occasion: he told her in his blandest manner that the peace of Europe was in the balance, that it could only be assured by a marriage between the King and the Infanta, but that had it not been so, they would have gladly welcomed her daughter as queen.

Swallowing her chagrin as best she could, the

From a sketch by R. P. Bonington.

ANNE OF AUSTRIA AND CARDINAL MAZARIN.

Princess was obliged to agree to everything that was laid before her, and beat a retreat in the most dignified manner possible. Princesse Marguerite won all hearts by her admirable behaviour under these trying circumstances. Her pride did not desert her and she showed no anger or impatience, but departed with her mother and their Court, leaving behind her a very pleasing impression.

CHAPTER XXVII

LOUIS XIV. AND MARIE MANCINI

SOON after all these exciting interviews had taken place the Cardinal fell ill with a bad attack of gout. The court, therefore, remained in Lyons, being unable to return to Paris. The Queen went every day to see him, while the King passed his time agreeably in making love to the fascinating Marie Mancini.

Anne was not only much displeased, but also rather alarmed; she disliked the girl personally, though she naturally did not wish to quarrel with the Cardinal's niece. Louis was still such a mere boy that he might be excused for his folly.

He used to whisper in her ear even in the Queen's presence, and they were never seen apart.

When Anne bade the company good-night the King used to escort Marie on her way home to the house where they were lodged. At first he used to put her into her coach, standing bareheaded on the steps as she drove away, waving a smiling adieu.

After a while he had his own carriage in readiness that he might follow and see her home in safety, and it was not long before he took his seat beside her.[1]

Anne was growing distinctly uneasy. She had hoped when Olympe was safely married that they had reached the end of that trouble, and now another and far more dangerous Mancini was on the scene, causing a public scandal. Anne's fervent desire was to see her son lead a sober, Christian life, so that he might be fit to aspire to the hand of her niece, while Louis, on the other hand, lived only for the passing amusement of the moment.

Mazarin chose to treat the matter lightly, though he could not have been altogether easy, for on the one side was the much-flattered Marie, with far less knowledge of the world than Olympe, coaxing her uncle to assist her in the matter, as she was sure she could be Queen without much difficulty, and on the other was Anne, with a face like a thunder-cloud, little inclined to treat the matter as a joke.

"I think, M. le Cardinal," she said one day in her very stateliest manner, "that it would be impossible for the King to behave in the dastardly manner that some people would have us believe. Should such a thought pass his mind, and were he tempted to offer so great an insult to Spain as to break off his engagement to the Infanta Marie-Thérèse, all France would rise up against him and you, and I should do the same."

[1] Amédée René, *Les Nièces de Mazarin*.

Mazarin smiled at this angry tirade, but with a touch of sarcasm; it was not often that Anne let herself go in this manner, especially in anything that concerned himself.

He laughed away the Queen's fears, and scorned the insinuations which were not worthy of being even considered. There were not wanting those who said the Cardinal had entertained the idea, but this was not at all in accordance with his usual policy, only it angered him to hear the Queen's slighting remarks on his favourite niece.

As he was just recovered from an attack of gout it is only natural to suppose that his temper was not very equable; but he saw the wisdom of putting a stop to this undignified affair so that he at least might be in the right. He determined to send away his nieces, at any rate, for a time, in charge of their governess, Madame de Venel.[1]

Once his plans were made he sought the presence of his King, and in his double capacity of Minister and former tutor taxed him with having carried this amiable weakness to lengths which impaired the royal dignity.

But Louis, whose infatuation was now at its height, refused to listen to reason, and swore he would marry Marie and none other.

A weaker man than Mazarin might have allowed himself to be dazzled by the greatness of this

[1] *Lettres inédites de Mazarin à Madame de Venel, pub. par Cheruel dans le Journal général d'Instruction publique.*

alliance, but he who dared everything was adamant on this occasion. This far-seeing man was never biassed by things of the moment; his mind, stretching into the future, saw how little such a marriage would redound to his credit, or bring about the successes he still aspired to.

He sternly refused his Sovereign's request.

After vainly beseeching his Minister to reconsider this matter, the King appeared to give in, and only craved for one last interview.

The boy was broken-hearted, or thought he was. The girl was playing a double game. Her juvenile lover had hardly touched her heart, but she stimulated profound grief in keeping with his tears. Again and again he embraced her, swearing that when he had attained full manhood neither Mazarin nor any one else should stand between him and his desires.

It was indeed a drama on a real stage, as the kingly lover held the hand of the ambitious beauty, and looked his whole soul into her eyes, while he vowed eternal fidelity; then she felt it was time to end the painful interview, and with tears streaming down her cheeks murmured, "You weep, and yet you are King and master," and with one long, last embrace they parted.[1]

The King, in a state of supreme depression, made no effort to hide his sorrow when he escorted the girls to their travelling coach, and then sorrowfully

---

[1] *Mémoires de Motteville.* Marie's phrase, often quoted, was ambiguous and daring—a challenge more than an act of submission.

re-joined his mother, who did her best to console him for his lost love.

It was decided the court should move to Fontainebleau to avoid the summer heat, while the Minister concluded his arrangements in Paris with Pimental. Diplomatic negotiations took so long in those days, when the facilities for communication were few, that it took from June to November of the same year to get the treaty signed.

It was settled that Mazarin should repair to the frontier for that purpose, and the Queen determined that they should all proceed to St. Jean-de-Luz together, and there the court could remain till the negotiations were concluded at the frontier, the Cardinal going in advance for that purpose.

While they were travelling by easy stages to Bordeaux, Louis implored his mother to allow him to go and bid Marie a last good-bye, as they would pass near the place where the Mademoiselles Mancini were residing. Anne could afford to be magnanimous now that she was within sight of the accomplishment of her desires, and she gave orders that Marie Mancini should await their arrival at St. Jean-d'Angély.

But there was little to fear from this interview, which was very different to the former one. Few tears were shed on either side. Louis, truth to tell, had his head full of his approaching marriage, and Marie knew that her empire over him was completely at an end, and accepted the situation philosophically. So ended this romance. The crown of France had never really been in danger, and the fair Mancini consoled herself speedily, while Louis spent the remainder of his long reign in falling under the influence of first one beautiful woman and then another.

CHAPTER XXVIII

TREATY OF PEACE AND MARRIAGE OF LOUIS XIV

ONCE more the scene is shifted to the Bidassoa, and forty-five years after the last royal pageant on the river's bank, much the same spectacle was to be re-enacted.

So long had the arrangements and negotiations taken that months had passed since the royal party had left Paris, but these preliminaries, though lengthy, were indispensable.

While they were still waiting in suspense, news was brought to the King and his mother which gave them great pleasure, and this was the intelligence that Charles II. of England had returned in triumph, and ascended the throne from which he had been driven. He was a great favourite with his aunt and cousin, and they rejoiced at his success.

On June 2, 1660, the Spanish King arrived at Fuenterrabia.

In the middle of the Bidassoa was a small island called "L'Ile des Faisans," and this had been converted into a more permanent boundary than had been the floating barges over which Anne and Elizabeth had passed to their respective thrones.

It was also called "L'Ile des Conférences." A building had been erected on it, with a hall in the centre as a throne-room, two royal chairs of state being placed so that one was on French territory and the other on that of Spain.

It was adorned in the most magnificent manner, and excited great curiosity. Owing to the formal etiquette existing in those days, it was judged necessary that the French court should remain at St. Jean-de-Luz, while the Spanish one was at St. Sebastian, and the King and his suite lodged at Fuenterrabia, therefore Anne and her brother did not meet, but received each other's envoys.

Louis also could only send tender inquiries after the health of the Infanta, to which she responded daily, with affectionate messages to her aunt.

Nevertheless, Louis took offence because none of the family had chosen to seek an interview with them, and when the day came for the marriage by proxy, he refused to allow Monsieur to go over to Fuenterrabia to witness the ceremony, though the boy begged hard to be allowed to go.

The Bishop of Pampeluna performed the service, which was held in the fine church on the top of the hill, and the mass having been said, Marie-Thérése stepped forward, and after the procuration of Louis had been read aloud she was called upon to give her consent. They were then pronounced man and wife, and she knelt before her father to receive his blessing.

The Infanta was a small, delicate-looking girl,

with very fair hair and blue eyes. She was too slender for the French taste, and they all agreed that had she had a more imposing presence, they would have admired her more.

Her Spanish court-dress also did not meet with their approval. The fashion in Spain for women was to wear their clothes very loose, and the dresses were cut very low at the back, without any kerchief, so that their shoulders were exposed. The sleeves were short, and there was a want of muslin and lace about the bodices. They wore monstrous hoops that made their skirts look like barrels flattened before and behind, and in walking this extraordinary machine swayed backwards and forwards.

A mass of false hair was worn, leaving the forehead high and uncovered. No wonder the little fair bride did not show to advantage in such a style.

Her dress was richly embroidered with a curious kind of talc, silver not being used for that purpose in Spain, and it was by no means an ornamental trimming. Her luxuriant hair was hidden under a white cap, which made her face look smaller and thinner than ever, and the French nobles wondered among themselves how their master would approve of his bride, though they admitted that she was not wanting in beauty if only she were properly dressed.[1]

The following day Anne, accompanied by one

[1] *Mémoires de Motteville.*

lady only, was to meet her brother and her new daughter-in-law on the Isle of Conference, but it was still against etiquette for Louis to meet his newly made wife, nor could the Kings of France and Spain come together till the day on which they were to sign the treaty of peace. Louis was, however, allowed to send her some of the crown jewels, which mission was entrusted to the Duc de Créquy.

Anne, with her warm, impulsive nature, ran forward to greet her brother, and wished to embrace him, but Philip held himself stiffly aloof, and only bowed gravely. Marie-Thérèse knelt before her aunt, who raised her in her arms and kissed her affectionately. Monsieur then came forward to greet his new relations, and the Cardinal (ever one of the family party) was warmly received by the King, who met him with an effusion he had not displayed towards his sister, and assured him that in his opinion Europe owed to Mazarin the peace about to be ratified. They seated themselves on the chairs, which were placed as near as possible on the line which marked the division between the two countries, and the long-parted brother and sister began a conversation which must have been most difficult and often painful.

The Cardinal chatted with the Ambassador Don Louis, and Monsieur entertained his sister-in-law.

While they were so engaged the Cardinal received a message from a stranger outside who craved admittance. He asked the King of Spain if he might venture to grant the request, and Philip politely agreed.

When the door was ajar, Anne coloured, for she saw who the intruder was, though he did not enter, but stood looking into the room; the new young Queen flushed up too, for she recognised at once that it was Louis himself.

The King of Spain relaxed his gravity for the first time, and smiled, saying to his sister, "I have a handsome son-in-law."

After gazing a few moments in silence, Louis, who had arranged with the Cardinal for this quaint interview to take place, departed as quietly as he had come.

Turenne and Condé, who were waiting outside, asked him eagerly what he thought of his bride. He replied that his first impression was that she was very plain, on account of her hideous dress and cap, but on closer inspection he saw that she was really pretty, and that she by no means displeased him.

The new Queen meanwhile was thanking Anne for the presents that had been brought to her by the Duc de Créquy.

"No, no, my dear," replied the Queen, "you must not thank me, for they are all from the King."

They were indeed magnificent, and besides tiaras and necklaces there were rings and bracelets, clocks, watches, gold boxes, and miniatures.

Mazarin's presents to the bride were a gold table service, two coaches, and twelve horses, with silver harness.

After this interview the King and his daughter entered their gorgeous State barge, and were rowed back to Fuenterrabia. On the way they saw Louis galloping along the pathway beside the river, with his plumed hat in his hand in the attitude of a devoted lover; upon which King Philip rose from his seat, and bowed profoundly, while the shy little Queen-Infanta looked on with admiring glances, greatly pleased at this gallantry displayed by her young husband. On Sunday, June 6, 1660, the peace was signed with all possible ceremony. Next day Anne and her son went in great state to the Hall of Conference to claim the Infanta.

The two royal families parted with much warmth and affection on both sides, and many tears were shed by the father and daughter.

As soon as the French court had returned to their own side of the river they placed the young Queen in a magnificent coach, and with a large escort of troops she was driven to St. Jean de Luz, where she was lodged in great state in her aunt's apartments. Etiquette required that she should at once retire for the night, and be seen no more, but she insisted on dining *en famille* with the Queen, the King, and Monsieur. She appeared in a charming *négligée*, with hair unbound, and every one went into raptures at her altered appearance.

The evening was passed in gay conversation, saddened at intervals by the recollection of the lonely King at Fuenterrabia.

Anne must have remembered keenly her own separation from her beloved father, but this bride had a far pleasanter greeting, without the dreadful loneliness which had been her portion when entering her new country.

The next day was spent pleasantly in looking at the presents, and showing off her trousseau to the Queen-Mother, as Anne was henceforth called, and the young couple attended Mass together.

June 9 was the great day for ratifying the marriage. The Queen was dressed by the Duchesse de Navailles, her mistress of the robes. She wore the royal mantle, embroidered with fleurs-de-lis, and with the diamond crown of France on her head looked very differently from what she had done at the preliminary ceremony.

The afternoon was spent in State functions, the King scattering largesse to the people, after the fashion of the time; they then dined in public, and repaired to the King's palace.

A few days later the royal party set out to return to Paris. They travelled rapidly, being anxious to reach the capital. The Queen-Mother and the Cardinal, as well as all the members of the royal family, remained with the King and Queen until they reached Fontainebleau. There the court halted for a time, but Anne left them, and went on to Paris. Mazarin was again suffering from gout, and she doubtless thought it best he should get back to his own house with as little delay as possible, and she did not care to leave him.

Besides this, her work beside her son was now at an end, and she felt she was no longer needed.

CHAPTER XXIX

DEATH OF MAZARIN

FOR some little time the Cardinal's health had been failing. His symptoms were greatly aggravated by the gout, and there were other complications which often caused him acute suffering.

During his absence from Paris he had constructed in his palace an appliance which may be regarded as the equivalent of a modern lift. It consisted of a chair worked by pulleys, and could be drawn through the floors by means of movable platforms or trap-doors, and was reckoned a great marvel of mechanical genius.

Mazarin had worked with even more than his usual energy over the promotion of the marriage and the peace, and now exhausted nature had its way, and a collapse ensued.

The King, who was living at Fontainebleau, used often to come into Paris to visit the sick Cardinal, and one day he asked him his advice on some point.

"Sire," replied Mazarin, "you ask counsel of a man who has lost his power of reasoning."

Louis, who all his life had loved his Minister, was so touched by this pathetic answer that he went out of the room without speaking, and shed tears of real sorrow in the gallery outside. Mazarin had been his tutor and his personal friend, and had guided him all his life, and he saw with grief that that great mind, however willing, was no longer capable of serving him.

When the serious nature of the Cardinal's illness became known, all the princes and nobles flocked to see him. The *Parlement* sent a deputation to him, an honour which had never been paid before to any Minister. Mazarin was much gratified and fully alive to the distinction shown to him, but his weakness and suffering made him indifferent to these earthly dignities, for the glories of the world were gradually fading away from him; he thought his end was approaching, but his fine constitution triumphed for a time, and he rallied considerably, to the satisfaction of his adherents and the intense joy of the Queen.

So life flowed back into its usual channels, and the court under the new young Queen was a scene of constant gaiety and rejoicing.

Having seen Louis happily married, Anne turned her attention to finding a suitable bride for her younger son, and determined this time to secure the little English princess of whom she was so fond. Henrietta Maria received this proposition with joy, and in spite of his youth the betrothal of Monsieur with his cousin took place without loss of time.[1]

---

[1] The marriage took place in 1661, and proved a very unhappy one. Monsieur took the title of Duc d'Orleans. This was the 4th royal house of that name.

The Cardinal was equally anxious to settle his nieces, for he knew well that, though he had rallied, his days were numbered. He sent for them to Paris, and lost no time in finding them suitable husbands. He consulted the horoscopes, a favourite habit of his, and a practice in which his niece Olympe de Soissons was proficient. At the Hôtel Soissons they encouraged astrologers and magic, which indeed was an inherited taste in the Mancini family.[1]

There had been a question of a marriage between Hortense and Charles II. of England. Henrietta Maria entertained the idea, attracted doubtless by the rumours as to the immense fortunes that the Cardinal's nieces would inherit, but the proposal was not carried into effect. Marie Mancini, who for a time had destroyed the peace of mind of the King, he betrothed to the Constable of Naples, Don Lorenzo, Prince de Colonna, and gave her a fortune of 100,000 livres and his fine house in Rome.[2]

The beautiful Hortense was married to the son of the Maréchal de la Meilleraye. He had long been in love with her, though originally it had been proposed that he should marry her elder sister Olympe, but the Cardinal had hitherto turned a deaf ear to his prayers, thinking the beauty of the family fit to mate with the highest of the land.

Whether Hortense herself pressed him to agree,

---

[1] *Mémoires de l'Abbé de Choisy.*
[2] Some amusing memoirs appeared in 1670, said to be from the pen of Marie Colonna, but they were condemned as apocryphal.

or whether the knowledge that the time was short had any weight with him, he consented to this match, on condition that La Meilleraye took the name and title of Duc de Mazarin. The wedding took place in the chapel of the Palace, before the King and royal family.

In after-years, as Duchesse de Mazarin, Hortense became notorious: she used to be called "the Queen of Paris," but her star arose after the real dynasty of the Mazarins had set.

There now only remained the little Marianne, and she eventually married the Duc de Bouillon, but that was long after her uncle's death.

Anne now saw with alarm that the Cardinal's malady was once more increasing and gaining ground. As his weakness grew he rarely left his own palace, but would sit, almost bent double, wrapped in a fur-lined dressing-gown, bowed down by the weight of his sufferings and regrets, his active mind still longing for occupation, his body daily becoming more helpless.

He would at times wander slowly and painfully down his long galleries among his art treasures, leaning on his stick, lost in sorrowful meditation on the vanity of human ambition. This painful picture of human greatness overpowered by human weakness was worthy of an artist's brush. The herald of that last enemy—the only one left—so soon to claim his own, faced the great Cardinal, and in combating this dread foe he had ceased to fear the rest.[1]

[1] La Borde, *Palais Mazarin.*

In February, 1661, Mazarin had been taken to Vincennes in the hopes that a change of air might benefit him; but all such measures were now unavailing, and on the 6th, feeling very ill, he despatched the Duc de Navailles to the King, to tell him that he was desirous to see him.

The Duke broke the news gently to his Majesty, and told him the physicians now feared the worst. Louis burst into tears and wept bitterly. He deplored the loss of the Cardinal and his untimely end.

"Could he but live four or five years more," he exclaimed, "I should be better able to govern my country. As it is I am not fit to do so, as I do not know where to turn, or whom to confide in."

He at once ordered the royal coaches to be got ready, and went to break the news to his mother. They started off for Vincennes together without loss of time.

Anne had little hope. Louis, who was young and sanguine, felt sure something might yet be done, especially as after their arrival the Cardinal took another turn for the better—but it was only the flicker of the candle.

Anne knew that human aid was now in vain, and she took her place by the bedside of the dying man. Silently she sat hour after hour, watching his laboured breathing and ministering to his wants.

Often he was irritable, and would treat her as if she were a sick nurse; once he exclaimed impatiently, " This woman will kill me with her importunities. Will she never leave me in peace?"[1] Weary with pain he seemed quite to forget that she was his Queen, and had been the adoration of his life; but with the sublime patience of a loving woman who forgives everything, Anne never flinched from her self-appointed task.

At times the dying Cardinal would look towards her with a glance of the old affection that had enriched her life, and murmur words of gratitude and love.

At dawn on March 7 Mazarin appeared to be sinking fast, and they sent word to the King that he had asked for the Holy Viaticum to be brought to him.

Louis would not awake his mother, who had fallen into a troubled sleep in the adjoining chamber, but sent at once to Paris with orders for the Archbishop to come and administer the last rites of the Church to the man who had held the highest dignities in her gift.

Mazarin, though very weak, was fully conscious, and prayed for divine mercy, and received the last sacraments in the presence of the King and the Queen-Mother. In spite of his calling, the life of Mazarin had by no means been one devoted to religion, nor had he ever expressed any veneration for the sacred mysteries; but at that solemn moment, when only a brief space divides a man from the unknown and the infinite, who can judge what passes between him

[1] *Mémoires de Montglat*, 1661.

and his Maker? The calm confidence displayed by the Cardinal in these last hours, and the courage with which he met the king of terrors, surely spoke of peace within.

On March 9 the palace was hung with black, and ten thousand masses were celebrated for the soul of Jules Mazarin, while in the darkened death-chamber Anne knelt, with streaming tears, in silent prayer, by the mortal remains of her beloved.

CHAPTER XXX

MAZARIN'S HEIRS

TWO centuries and a half divide that moment from the present, and this interval renders it impossible to estimate rightly the characters of the eminent men or women whose lives we are narrating.

Voltaire said of Mazarin, "C'est à ses actions de parler," and certainly his actions had shown the greatness of his talents.

His motto was, "Time, and myself.' Arrogant and self-assertive as these words are, they also point to the great nature that was sufficient to itself, and though his defects were many and obvious, it is impossible to deny his consistent patriotism, and the immense services he rendered to France by strengthening its position both at home and abroad.

The besetting vice of this celebrated statesman was his love of money, which was insatiable; but to counterbalance this rapacity, Mazarin possessed a refined and liberal taste for learning and the arts, and left behind him three conspicuous and lasting monuments of his munificence—the "Collége des Quatre Nations" (now the Institute of France), the magnificent "Mazarino" library, and the "Académie" of painting and sculpture.

The "Collége" was intended to educate natives of those provinces which had been added to the country by Richelieu and himself—Roussillon, Alsace, Artois, and Pinerolo. The rising generation was to be brought up in Paris, and return to spread French culture and interests in their own homes. It was a bequest worthy of the statesman whose diplomacy had been so successful in extending the frontier of France.

The many temptations, due to his exalted position and to the age in which he lived, which assailed Mazarin, render it difficult to get at a just estimate of his character, but his greatness none can gainsay, and the honours rendered to him in death point to the opinion in which he was held.

The lying-in-state of the Cardinal gave thousands of people the opportunity of gazing once more on those well-known classic features, serene and beautiful even in death. The court wore mourning, an honour which had never before been paid to a subject, for a king only wears black for near relations or brother sovereigns.[1]

But though this token of love and respect was shown to Mazarin's memory, and he was mourned in high places, not much grief was exhibited among the world at large. The lion was dead, and the people had nothing more to fear from him.

The good folk of Paris, who had run after the Minister in his lifetime, and the flatterers who had surrounded him, ceased to have any further interest;

[1] *Mémoires de Motteville.*

indeed, they were now busy in writing and repeating lampoons and witty rhymes, for this last form of satire was a very favourite one in that and succeeding centuries, and neither age nor sex was ever sacred from it. These verses were withering, often pointless, coarse, and malicious, and they spared neither the living nor the dead.

The Queen-Mother, though still in their midst, was a fitting object for their senseless verses, while the Cardinal's foibles and generosities alike served to point and adorn the scurrilous abuse.[1]

Every man now began to tell his neighbour that Mazarin had been their curse; they discovered that he had been the most hated person in the kingdom, and the source of all their woes, and soon the fickle crowd poured out abuse over the very remains of the dead Cardinal.

The first few weeks after his death were entirely occupied in discussing the enormous wealth he had left behind him. He had accumulated a private fortune amounting to fifty millions of francs, representing at least double that sum according to the present value of money.

Though he had disinherited his surviving nephew, and made the husband of Hortense his heir, he left young Mancini the principality of Ferrati in Italy.

[1] " Mazarin sortit de Mazare
Aussi pauvre que Lazare,
Réduit à la nécessité ;
Mais par les soins d'Anne d'Autriche,
Ce Lazare ressuscité
Est mort comme le mauvais riche."
Mémoires de Montglat.

He left large fortunes to his nieces—the Princesse de Conti, the Duchesse de Modena, the Princesse de Colonna, and the Comtesse de Soissons, and 200,000 ecus for the little Marianne, the youngest.[1]

But, as was said before, the lion's share fell to Hortense, who inherited the Palais Mazarin with all its art treasures as well as an immense fortune. Most likely this was because he had selected her to carry on his name.

To his great-nephews, the children of the Duchesse de Mercœur, he left large sums, and appointed bishoprics and government offices for all those who had served him faithfully.

How this enormous fortune was accumulated has never been clearly ascertained. Besides his lucrative appointments and his numerous abbayes, he had immense perquisites appertaining to his post of Minister, and large percentages from contracts for the army, the admiralty, the ambassadors, and the royal household. De Tellier explains his huge fortune by saying it was not taken from the people, but was entirely due to successful speculations, and his passion for play with high stakes was well known.

Be that as it may, it is at least certain that the Cardinal's two great passions in life were glory and riches, and he had worked hard to achieve both.[1] It was a hopeless task to silence public opinion— the world at large preferred to think that Mazarin's wealth was ill-gotten.

[1] *Lettres de Colbert.*

His personal legacies to the royal family were more of the nature of mementos. To the King he left eighteen huge diamonds, and to the Queen a magnificent parure. To Monsieur he left costly emeralds, while to Anne he bequeathed one large diamond, perhaps one that he always wore, and which would thus be doubly precious to her.

Louis deeply and personally regretted him, though some writers, regardless of the loving care and sorrow he displayed during Mazarin's illness, tried to make out that the King rejoiced at his Minister's death.[1] There was, however, great truth in the saying that his reign really only began when the Cardinal was laid in his tomb. The aptitude displayed by Louis in taking up the reins of government surprised those who had hitherto looked upon him as a mere careless boy; but they forgot whose hand had guided his youth, whose genius had taught him how to govern, and whose mighty talent had cleared the way for the long and victorious reign of the "Grand Monarque."

Life at court soon began to change also; the intriguing beauties who had reigned there so long passed away to make room for younger and equally frail charmers. The Duchesse de Longueville on becoming a widow returned to Paris and settled herself with her children near the Hôtel Sablé, where the Marquise de Sablé held a salon as famous as the Hôtel Rambouillet of a later date.

[1] *Mémoires de Motteville. Mémoires de Montglat.*

Whether it was want of fortune or want of health, Madame de Longueville left the scenes of court gaiety and intrigues in which she could no longer take a place, and joined the circle of " Précieuses" and " Littéraires" who flocked to this salon.

The Duchesse de Chevreuse lived to the age of seventy-nine. Before she died she saw all she had either loved or hated pass away—Richelieu, Louis XIII., Mazarin, Anne, Henrietta Maria, Chateauneuf, Charles of Lorraine, and many others. She became very devout at the end, as did so many of the great ladies in those days when the world and its pleasures had receded from them, and established herself in a modest little house at Gagny near the Convent de Chelles, where she died in the odour of sanctity, her long list of former iniquities being overlooked by virtue of the Christian manner in which her last hours were spent.[1]

---

[1] Her epitaph was as follows:

"Cy gist Marie de Rohan, Duchesse de Chevreuse, fille de' Hercule de Rohan, Duc de Montbazon. Elle avait epousé en premières noces, Charles d'Albert Duc de Luynes, pair et Connestable de France et en secondes noces, Claude de Lorraine, Duc de Chevreuse.

"L'humilité ayant fait mourir, dans son cœur toute la grandeur du siècle, elle defendit que l'on fit revivre à sa mort la moindre marque de sa grandeur, qu'elle voulut achever d'ensevelir sous la simplicité de cette tombe, ayant ordonné qu'on l'entérrat dans la paroisse de Gagny ou elle este morte à l'age de 79, 12 Août 1679."

Abbé de Bœuf, *Histoire du Diocèse de Paris*, chap. vi. p. 130.

CHAPTER XXXI

CONCLUSION

ANNE lived for five years after Mazarin's death. Not only did she lose the chief interest of her life, but also that phase of her career with which this book is mainly concerned was ended by his death; the latter portion of Anne's life belongs, strictly speaking, to the history of Louis XIV.

As Queen-Mother she took no part in the affairs of the nation. She had the happiness before her end of seeing the Dauphin born, as well as a second son, and of being assured that her dearly beloved Louis had heirs to his throne.

The daughter-in-law she had welcomed so kindly was a comfort and solace to her declining years, and she lived to see peace and tranquillity in France taking the place of the many revolts and civil wars through which she had struggled during her long regency.

The rest and quiet she had so long wished for were hers at last. Let us hope that in this leisure she had some recompense for the stormy life she had led at times, and the many self-sacrifices of her earlier days, for there is no doubt she must have often done violence to herself when she had to forgo any of the practices so dear to her to suit the convenience or pleasures of others.

But the calm and peaceful closing years soon doomed her to yet one more painful struggle. In 1663 a malignant and loathsome disease assailed her, and she was pronounced to be suffering from cancer.

For three long years she bore her illness with the patience of a saint. Her faithful chronicler, Madame de Motteville, gives a long detailed account of her terrible illness till death at last brought her peace, January 20, 1666. So ended the life of Anne of Austria, whose place in history is chiefly owing to her having been the mother of the great King Louis XIV. and Queen-Regent of France for so many years.

It would be a misnomer to call her a great Queen, for she had no special aptitude for the burden of government early laid upon her, and she never really overcame her natural idleness of disposition. Through the long years of her reign she had been only the faithful echo of the voice that guided her, and a willing disciple of that master mind so far wiser than her own. Perhaps in that it may be said her wisdom lay, for she ever effaced herself, giving place to the man she loved.

Her prudence and firmness, on many a trying occasion, did her honour, and to her last hour she deserved the love and gratitude of her son. Her piety and devotion to her Church, of which the fine convent of Val-de-Grace was an outward pledge, are well known, and have caused her memory to live in the hearts of the faithful.

A neglected wife, and, though a mother, having but young children who could be no support to her, her life would have been lonely indeed save for the great and enduring affection that entered into it.

What the tie was that bound Anne and Mazarin the world never knew, and in the face of so much and such conflicting evidence the question is perhaps best left unanswered. That the Queen loved the Cardinal with all the devotion of an adoring woman there is no doubt, and the Cardinal returned that devotion as much as it was in his somewhat cold and self-seeking nature. When death came and sundered the lives which for so long had been bound up in each other, the one who was left knew that life held nothing more for her, and she did not survive him many years.

Perhaps what brings her most vividly before us as a real and living woman, with the frailties and passions common to all, is this very human weakness, and the chief interest we feel in her life arises from the record of the steadfast love that existed between this illustrious Queen and the great Italian Cardinal.

FINIS

INDEX

Ancre, Maréchal d', 16
Anjou, Philippe Duc d', 67 ; Petit Monsieur, 95, 111, 126, 153, 243, 251
Anna, Infanta of Spain, 2-9
Anne of Austria (wife of Philippe II.), 3
Anne of Austria (Queen of France), 13 ; affair with Buckingham, 18-25 ; intrigues, 28, 29 ; her beauty, 38 ; "Coup de Compiègne," 41 ; birth of Dauphin, 66 ; her daily life, 94-98 ; intimacy with Mazarin, 107 ; flight to St. Germains, 153 ; ceases to be Regent, 213 ; her death, 264

Balthazar, Don, 118
Barberini, Cardinal, 63
Bartet, M., 200, 202
Bassompierre, Maréchal de, 47
Beaufort, Duc de, 17, 86, 120, 158, 166, 181, 206
Beaumont, Abbé de, 117, 118
—— Mlle. de, 97, 152
Beauvais, Bishop, 81
—— Madame, 133, 168
Bellegarde, Duc de, 17
Beringhen, M. de, 96, 152
Bertaud, Madame, 14
Blancmesnil, M., 144
Bouillon, Duc de, 69
Bourbon, Princesse de, 86
Bregi, Ambassadeur de, 113
—— Madame de, 97

Brienne, Comte de, 100, 217
—— Madame de, 123
Broussel, 144-147
Brun, Le, 203
Buckingham, George Villiers, Duke of, 18, 19, 21, 24, 25, 31, 32, 33

Caudale, Duc de, 167
Carigman, Princesse de, 223
Cinq Mars, Marquis de, 69, 70
Chandenier, Marquis de, 96, 143
Chalais, Marquis de, 27, 30
Charles I., King of England, 17, 19, 159
Charles of Lorraine, 47, 216
Charost, Comte de, 143
Chateauneuf, M. de, 46, 48, 74-100, 213
Charton, M., 144
Châtillon, Duc de, 85
—— Madame de, 215
Chauvigny, M. de, 191
Chavigny, M. de, 69, 74
Chevreuse, Duc de, 163
—— Duchesse de, 16 ; friendship with Anne, 20 ; evil influence, 25 ; mischief-maker, 31 ; flight to Spain, 52, 54 ; exiled again, 74 ; returns to France, 82 ; intrigue, 84-93 ; returns to Paris, 163, 164 ; her death, 262
—— Mlle. de, 209
Coetqueen, Marquis de, 90
Colbert, 232
Coligny, M. de, 85, 91

INDEX

267

Cominges, M. de, 96, 144
Condé, Prince de, 7, 75, 103, 171, 213, 216
—— Princesse de, 153
Conté, Princesse de, 22
Conti, Prince de, 155, 157, 181, 209, 222

Elbœuf, Duc de, 112
Elisabeth, Madame, 2
Enghien, Duc d', 103
Estefana, Donna, 4

Fenton, 33
Ferdinand I., 1
Foix, 93
Fleix, Comtesse dè, 175

Gesvres, Marquis de, 142
Gonzague, Marie de, 38, 70
Grammont, Duc de, 104
Guébriant, Maréchale de, 113
Guéménee, Princesse de, 38, 108, 115, 179
Grimaldi, 128
Guise, Duc de, 5, 10, 91
—— Mlle. de, 38

Harcourt, Comtesse de, 206
Haro, Don Louis de, 227
Hauteville, Madame de, 56
—— Mlle. de, 38
Henri IV., 2
Henrietta Maria, 17, 22, 25, 37, 102, 103, 225, 251
Herouard, M., 8

Jabach, M., 221
Jars, Chevalier de, 45, 51, 96
Jarzé, M., 142–148
—— Marquis de, 165, 168, 170
Jouvigni, M. de, 27
Joyeuse, Duc de, 106

Ladislas, King of Poland, 108, 115
Laffemas, 48, 51

Lannoi, Comtesse de, 23
Lenore, Signora, 99
Lequier, Chancellor, 146
Longueville, Duc de, 86, 181
—— Duchesse de, 84, 93, 155, 156, 161, 175, 181, 184, 261
Louis XII., 1
Louis XIII., 2, 7, 9, 12, 74
Louis XIV., 66; accession, 75; childhood, 95; attends *Parlement*, 105; Polish wedding, 112; small-pox, 125; attends Notre Dame, 142; state entry, 173, 212; love for Marie Mancini, 236, 241; his marriage, 248
Luynes, Duc de, 9–15, 16
—— Duchesse de, 15

Mancini, Madame, 62, 224
—— Olympe, 137, 222, 224
—— Marie, 225, 226, 236, 241, 252
—— Hortense, 225, 252, 289
Marie-Thérèse, 238, 244, 249
Marsillac, Princesse de, 175, 178
Martinozzi, 137, 224
Mazarin, Cardinal, 59; appointed minister, 76; "Petit Conseil," 79; friendship with Anne, 82; purchase of palace, 128; dominion over the Queen, 135; arrival of his nieces, 136; his flight, 188; letters to the Queen, 194–208; triumphant return, 217; his death, 256; his last will, 258
Mazarin, Duc de, 253
Mazarino, Pietro, 59
Medici, Marie de', 11, 16, 26, 39, 41–44
Meilleraye, Maréchal de, 222, 252
Mercœur, Duc de, 162, 174, 211
—— Duchesse de, 224, 260
Montbazon, Duchesse de, 37, 84, 93
——Mlle. de, 177, 178
Montglat, Madame de, 7
Moissens, M. de, 177
Molé, M., 107

INDEX

Montmorency, Duc de, 17
Montpensier, Mlle. de, 26

Navailles, Duc de, 254
—— Duchesse de, 214

Orleans, Duc d', 75, 77, 78, 103, 106, 112, 137, 140, 185
—— Duchesse d', 153, 154
—— Mlle. d', 120, 153
Orsini, Portia, 62

Palatine, Princesse, 108, 133
Philip III., 3
Philip IV., 2, 118, 245
Pimental, Don, 231
Pons, Madame de, 175, 177
—— Mlle. de, 121
Porte, La, 55, 57, 122, 123
Posmane, Palatin de, 110

Urban VIII., 71, 133

Renard, 87
Retz, Duc de, 166
—— Cardinal de, 31, 77, 83–101
Richelieu, Cardinal, 14; siege of La Rochelle, 32, 33; passion for Anne, 35; hatred of Marie de' Medici, 39; dislike of Madame de Chevreuse, 45; his insolence, 55; his triumph, 57; his death, 71; his relations, 80
Rivière, Abbé de la, 112–175

Rochefoucauld, Comte de, 48, 52, 73
Rohan, Duchesse de, 92
—— Marie de, 16
—— Mlle. de, 38
Romanelli, 128
Ruffalini, Ortensia, 59
Ruvigny, 165

Sablé, Marquise de, 17, 261
Saint Martin, Mlle. de, 121
Savoy, Princess Marguerite of, 229–235
Scarron, 63
Senacé, Marquise de, 81, 93, 175
Sequier, Chancellor, 37
Soissons, Comte de, 223

Tellier, M. de, 217, 260
Thou, M. de, 70
Trêmes, Comte de, 142
Tremouille, Comtesse de, 151–177
Tubœuf, President, 127
Turennes, Maréchal, 103, 159, 216

Vautier, M., 47
Vendôme, Duc de, 75–78, 162
—— Mlle. de, 38
Venel, Madame de, 230
Vieuville, Marquis de, 47
Vigneul, 180
Villequier, Marquis de, 143
Villeroy, Marquis de, 118
Vincent, Père, 133

Printed by Hazell, Watson & Viney, Ld., London and Aylesbury.

Dec. 12

YC 74044

LIBRARY USE
RETURN TO DESK FROM WHICH BORROWED
LOAN DEPT.

THIS BOOK IS DUE BEFORE CLOSING TIME ON LAST DATE STAMPED BELOW

LIBRARY USE	
LIBRARY USE	
RECEIVED DEC 29 '66 -3 PM LOAN DEPT.	

LD 62A–50m-7,'65
(F5756s10)9412A

General Library
University of California
Berkeley

CPSIA information can be obtained
at www.ICGtesting.com
Printed in the USA
FSOW03n2000010716
22316FS